974.3   Mitchell, Don
MI
         Living upcountry

$12.95

DATE		
SE 8'88		
OC 16'88		
FE 15'91		
AP 6'91		
JE 26 91		
MY 3'93		
MAY 3 0 '06		
FE 1 8		
SE 1 2 07		

Living UpCountry

A PILGRIM'S PROGRESS

Other Books by Don Mitchell

Living UpCountry

A Pilgrim's Progress

by Don Mitchell

YANKEE® BOOKS

a division of
Yankee Publishing Incorporated
Dublin, New Hampshire

To George and Lauraine Warfield

Portions of this book, in a somewhat different form, first appeared in *Boston* magazine under the column head "R.F.D."

First Edition
Copyright 1986 by Don Mitchell
Printed in the United States of America

Library of Congress Catalog Card Number: 86-50091
ISBN: 0-89909-100-8

Designed by Jill Shaffer
Illustrations by Carl Kirkpatrick

Contents

Author's Note

A number of readers of *Moving UpCountry*
have asked to know the name of the author's
wife. Her name is Cheryl, and the author
owes her a great deal, but the characterization of the author's wife in these essays
has only the most tangential relation to the
author's wife's character. The author was
trained as a novelist, a teller of stories, and
it's hard for even a middle-aged dog to learn
new tricks. Nothing in the present collection
of essays is meant to be taken as strictly
factual; on the other hand, the author hopes
that he has told the truth.

CHAPTER ONE

What Do the Simple Folk Do?

ALL TOO OFTEN, URBANITES WHO move upcountry plan to realize substantial savings in their domestic economies. After all, aren't rural bumpkins *poor?* And don't they get by somehow? Yes, and yes again; but the locals are adept at certain life-skills that the newcomers lack, and do not aspire to learn. The locals, for example, keep their Valiants and Novas strapped together — running, too — with rusty hairpins and discarded baling twine. Saabs and BMWs do not respond well to such treatment.

Groceries from the typical supermarket in Vermont cost as much as groceries in New Jersey — or, most likely, *more.* Professionals like to charge professional-type fees whether they do business in White River Junction or White Plains. Fuel bills, tax bills, electric bills, insurance — all can be surprisingly upscale, even in a decidedly cold and rural place. Generally speaking, the good life in the New England sticks can be about as costly as the good life in considerably more civilized places.

One area, however, where authentic bargains do exist is in the realm of entertainment. This is primarily because the rural Yan-

7

kee's calendar includes vast stretches of time during which there is damn little to do. Some mistake this condition of our lives for simple boredom — and for some, I do not doubt, it *is* boredom incarnate — but even while apparently nothing is going on, the acclimated immigrant to our society can manage to feel splendidly entertained.

Mud season, for example, turns the most innocent gestures toward mobility into Herculean challenges. A landscape filled with vehicles sunk up to their axles and pedestrians sunk up well beyond their ankles is nothing if not entertaining. Spring makes sportsmen of us all. And there are those real sportsmen to enjoy each autumn, too, when for sixteen days ordinary routine is suspended as we celebrate the ancient Festival of the Deer. You needn't even leave your house to feel totally involved.

Then there is the sense of occasion that people with not enough to do bring to otherwise commonplace or mildly shabby events. It is not a pile of garbage set out under some dead elm, it is a Huge Five-Family Lawn Sale!! Today!! Till Everything Is Sold!! The seasoned Yankee will approach such a happening with the spirit of adventure.

The bottom line is, those of us who would be entertained are thrown back on our own resources. Money need not be one of them — seldom is. But in time one learns how to create a good time, whether in a grown-up bash of capture the flag in a neighbor's rock-strewn woodlot, or in quiet evenings reading plays aloud by well-stoked woodstoves, or in dining with distinction on some distant mountaintop. High art is in short supply, but low art is abundant and extremely entertaining once one gets the hang of it. Here, then, are a few specimen Good Times for the simple folk.

• Buck Fever

I hadn't lived long in Vermont when folks began to ask me if I planned to do some deer hunting. It was an appalling question. I was a pacifist; I had just finished a two-year stint of alternative service to the Vietnam draft. The last thing I wanted to do was go find a deer and shoot it.

I did not preach, Bambi-like, to my neighbor sportsmen. I was not out proselytizing for nonviolence. People were amazed, however, to learn that I owned no rifle. Didn't even *want* to own one.

Hadn't even fired a gun since Merit Badge days in the Boy Scouts. I had moved into a culture where grown men shoot animals as basic recreation, like bowling leagues or softball teams in the suburbs. And deer season, plainly, was the lofty pinnacle of their hunting experience: one of those special celebrations that makes life worth living.

After several of these deer-hunting conversations, I could place the concept in a rational — a conservationist — perspective. I was not a fanatic defender of wildlife. I understood that nature could run amok. With few natural predators, the population of an adapted species like the white-tailed deer in a habitat like Vermont could burgeon to the point where there were simply no benefits. Unchecked, the deer would soon overwhelm their upland food supply. Then thousands upon thousands of scrawny, malnour-ished, disease-prone does and bucks would shuffle out of the hills to damage farmers' crops and trees. Licensing the citizenry to kill off a portion of the deer herd each November — after breeding season, but before the rigors of hard winter — seemed a reason-able way to keep nature in balance.

Once I understood the structure of deer hunting, another compelling reason emerged for supporting it. Vermont's Fish and Wildlife Department, whose responsibilities are legion and whose budget is not small, can raise a lot of dough by selling hunting licenses to out-of-staters at sixty bucks a throw. (Vermonters them-selves shell out only eight dollars.) In an upbeat brochure de-signed to bag the out-of-staters, Vermont points out that hunters here have substantially better chances — based on many years of record-keeping — of taking a deer in this state than elsewhere in New England. Advertising? Sure, but I could well appreciate the wisdom of getting sportsmen from, say, Massachusetts to under-write the costs of Vermont's fish and wildlife programs.

So much for rationales. When my first November in Vermont rolled around, I realized immediately that deer season operates at the level of some primordial throb that mocks any towers of reason built to justify it. Deer season has precisely the character of an arcane religious festival in an alien culture; no doubt it is one of those magical glues that somehow make for social cohesion in a semicivilized place.

It lasts for sixteen days, beginning twelve days before Thanksgiving, any given year. You know it has begun because nearly all men — and many women — cease to do what they would ordinarily be doing. Lawyers and shopkeepers, plumbers and mechanics all shutter their doors behind GONE HUNTING signs. Why, even the landfill that we drive to with our household garbage has a sign at its entrance: "Open Every Day Except Christmas, New Year's, and the First Day of Deer Season." Now, *that* puts some other feast days into sharp relief.

Furthermore, as any good cultural anthropologist would immediately note, the Festival of the Deer requires all citizens to don special ceremonial garments. Hunter's red, red plaid, blaze orange from head to foot. And not just hunters deck themselves out in these bright, gaudy costumes: thoughtful parents do not let their children out the front door without the required clothes. Even dogs are getting scarves. Anything that moves and is not red is in profound danger.

The most telling evidence, however, of the cathartic and regenerative role that deer season plays in our cultural drama is that with it comes a wholesale suspension of the private property rights that people scrupulously observe at all other times of the year. I noticed this immediately on opening day of my first deer season here. It was scarcely dawn, and I awoke to hear a number of pickup trucks park by the roadside not far from my house. Doors swung open and slammed shut; voices whispered; by the time I pulled my jeans on, half a dozen gunslingers had fanned out across my peaceful little valley.

"Aren't they supposed to ask your permission?" my wife demanded. "Aren't they trespassing?"

I supposed they were. But when I saw their numbers — six armed men! — I quickly decided not to play Sheriff of Nottingham. "Look," I said, "the land's not posted."

"Maybe you *should* post it."

"Maybe." Except that then, I thought, I *would* have to drive stray sportsmen from my valley. It was the sort of confrontation I did not mind ducking. As I watched, each member of the merry band stationed himself at a regular interval along the stream that drains my farm. Beyond the stream is scruffy woodlot, then a low, forested mountain. What I couldn't see — yet — were the nine *other* hunters on the back side of that rocky foothill, marching toward their brethren and chasing any hapless deer down into their gunsights.

This flush-and-stakeout strategy for hunting the elusive whitetail was completely different from the solitary, stalking marksmen that I had expected. This was ganging up; this was manifestly unfair to the deer involved. After several hours, though, it turned out that there *were* no deer involved. The hill had yielded nothing. Spying out our own windows onto our own property, my wife and I watched the posse reassemble and drive off. Buckless.

It was nearly ten o'clock on what, I now expected, would be a sorely trying day. I told my wife: "I think I'll run out to the liquor store."

"Me too!" she cried. "Don't leave me here!"

So we swathed ourselves in red and made a beeline for the car without getting fired upon. Our local liquor store is Dick and Glenda's, in Vergennes, which also just happens to be a sporting goods store. This makes it one of New England's few liquor stores — I feel certain about this — that a man can walk into with a .30-.30 deer rifle to pick up a fifth of George Dickel. It is a startling sight. And deer hunters, I couldn't help from noticing that chilly morning, are an inordinately thirsty lot who seem to specialize in high-proof beverages.

My wife and I padded to the back of the store — quiet, innocuous, making no waves — and seized upon a half gallon of cream sherry. Then, at the cash register, my eye came to rest on stacks of two thick brochures published at the state's expense. One was Vermont's official Alcohol Beverage Price List; the other, put out by the Agency of Environmental Conservation, was the Digest of Fish and Wildlife Laws. Since both were free, I picked up one of each and placed them in my bag. Then we beat a hasty retreat to our besieged estate.

Hunkered down at the kitchen table, trying to get relaxed, my wife read out excerpts from the fish and game book while I studied alcoholic beverage prices. "Get this: '*Showing License on Demand.* A person who is hunting or fishing shall show licenses immediately upon demand of State Game Wardens, other officers, and the *owner of the land* upon which the person is hunting or fishing. *Persons must leave* the land immediately on demand of the owner, *whether the land is posted or not.*'"

"So?"

"So all you had to do was tell those guys to leave."

"There were *fifteen* of them, dear. With *rifles*."

"But the law is on your side."

"Nice to know," I said. "Now, look at this — there's a column here where every brand of booze is *unit priced!*"

"No fooling?"

"Gilbey's vodka, 16.6 cents an ounce. Smirnoff, 26.8 cents. Wolfschmidt . . . "

"What a state this is! Devoted to the cause of cheap drunks. Least-cost drunks, I mean."

We swapped booklets. She began checking on what different sherries cost per ounce, and I turned up such arcane rules as that paraplegics, when properly certified by the commissioner of Fish and Wildlife, were allowed to hunt while sitting in their motor vehicles. Here was, manifestly, a sport for everybody.

"Damn," my wife said testily. "We missed out on the cheapest sherry."

Tires squealed on the road, and another group of hunters climbed out, checked their ammo, and began negotiating my pasture fence. "Here we go again," I said.

"Just walk out there and ask to see their licenses."

"No way."

"They're not going to shoot you."

I was not so sure. But, fortified with not-quite-least-cost courage, I pulled on my reds and staggered out the door. The hunters were staggering, too, so we shared a measure of common ground. "Afternoon," I said politely. "You fellows deer-hunting?"

They looked at me as though I'd just arrived from Mars. "Yeah," said one at last. "You seen any bucks up on that ridge?"

"Nope," I said. "And a whole bunch of hunters came up empty there this morning."

An older man spat on the ground. "There's deer up there, all right. Took a nice ten-pointer on that ridge in fifty-seven."

"Don't forget Armand Marcotte's buck in sixty-four, either," pointed out another. "Rack on that buck! How much did it dress?"

"Hunnert fifteen, anyway."

"By Jesus."

I was mildly astounded, as at men who know their baseball stats. "How long have you guys been hunting here?" I asked.

The old one thought back. "Thirty years, anyway. Guess I know those woods up there."

"Well," I said, "I'm the new landowner. And I ... I don't suppose I'm going to try to stop you."

They weaved off to beat the bushes, and I weaved back to tell my wife about the niceties of life in a traditional society. None of those Robin Hoods found that year's buck on my ridge, either.

Every night of deer season, a special radio program broadcasts the names of that day's successful hunters, the weights and rack sizes of their kills, and sage advice about where the big ones are being taken. All this information comes out in the weekly papers, too, creating heroes out of otherwise perfectly ordinary citizens. And to see one's photo right there on page 1, posed proudly over some enormous and quite dead white-tailed deer — this is, I imagine, the very highest glory a Vermonter can hope to achieve.

After its explosive start, buck fever settles down to a dull roar that slowly builds as Thanksgiving Day approaches. We protect the fine conceit that all this hoopla is about putting meat on the table, after all. But *after* Thanksgiving, those who have not found their deer enter an increasingly frenzied state. In this now-or-never phase of the season, more and more nondeer are mistakenly targeted; over the years I have read of several cows, horses, sheep, and even one bulldozer being thus fired upon. But when it is over, it is over; life returns to normal thirty minutes after the sunset of the sixteenth day.

Another year, a couple of hunters *did* take a buck here. They had to drag it out down a rocky cliff and through a swamp; to think that meat so handled would be eaten by human beings made the federal food and drug laws seem phenomenally stringent. But I went to watch them load the animal atop their car to take it to the nearest deer reporting station.

"First buck taken here in several years," I told the sportsmen.

"Guess so. Place was due for it."

"Glad you never posted this place," said his companion. "Glad somebody who doesn't hunt *understands* deer hunting."

"Oh, I understand," I said. "I understand it's something bigger than I am. Why, even sitting up there in my house, I feel part of it. And in my own quiet way, I do enjoy it."

This speech didn't grab them. "Know what I say?" said the first one, strapping a near-rigid leg to the cargo rack on his car roof. "I just say, 'If your land's posted, buddy, stay to hell off mine!'"

Sort of live and let live, in a context of determined carnage. That's the way it is here. And when I chance to flush a deer while tramping in the upper woodlot, I explain the same to him. I explain: Get lost, pal.

• Mud Capades

One of my last adventures in real life — before settling down to try to pass as a Vermonter — was to ride a slow, decrepit, overbooked train from Istanbul to Austria. It was early April. Out the grimy window of our cramped compartment, half a dozen Turks and I watched sullen, dispirited farmers struggling to pick their feet up out of an endless sea of mud. Bulgarians and Yugoslavians dressed in drab, mended garments, leather boots weighed down with globs of wet, sticky soil. What a compelling image, I thought, for the apparent dreariness of rural peasant life behind the Iron Curtain.

Roughly two weeks later, my wife and I took possession of the Vermont farm that we had acquired nearly a year before. I remember flinging wide the rustic pasture gate, and then aiming our eager sports car toward the distant cedar grove where we planned to pitch a tent. But the car never got within a quarter mile of that campsite; ten yards off the road, my capitalist Porsche hunkered down in slippery clay and soon was swallowed past its chrome wheel covers. Climbing out, and cursing loudly, I realized something most significant: rural communists have no monopoly on mud. Mud is shared by everyone who lives beyond the reach of pavement.

Mud, I learned soon enough, is an entire *season* in Vermont — of which "spring" is but the final weekend, at most. At a time when young men's thoughts, in other regions, turn to love, Vermonters annually watch three implacable phenomena conspire to turn verdant fields to bottomless yuck. First there is the melting of snow, sometimes several packed feet of the stuff. Second is the gradual thawing, from the top down, of soils that can be frozen to a depth of four feet. Third are the April showers of which flower gardeners like to make light. Put these three natural forces in league, and the consequences strain an outsider's credulity.

Did I say our mud was bottomless? It is *not*, at first — and therein lies much of our problem. Until frost works completely out of subsoils, water near the surface simply has no way to percolate into the ground; in the highly expansive clay soils for which Vermont is famous, this creates a colloidal glop above the frost line that has the adhesive properties — the approximate color, too — of peanut butter. Trying to scrape the stuff off one's boots — or off one's shovel, for that matter — is like trying to lick creamy smooth Jif off one's coated palate. You can never get it all.

Then, one day, the subsoil thaws. Then our mud is bottomless. It was in this terminal stage of mud season when I sunk my Porsche, and I hadn't spun my wheels for very long before a neighbor stopped. With a winch on his pickup truck. "Headed somewhere?" he asked pithily.

I introduced myself. He did not question my assertion that I was the out-of-stater who had bought this muddy acreage; my license plate — above water, fortunately — seemed sufficient to explain what my car was doing there, mired as only a novice at mud could mire his vehicle.

"Winch ought to pull you out," he offered.

"Could you?"

"Sure. No trouble." He hooked the steel cable from the winch to my car frame, and soon the Porsche was back on terra firma. Then he offered to drive my wife and me and our camping gear to the distant site that our car would never reach.

"How?" I asked, incredulous.

He pointed out some of the finer features of his truck. "Four-wheel drive. Low range. Off-road tires. Course, I'm apt to leave some ruts." He grinned. "But we ought to get there."

"No, thanks," I said. "I don't mind hiking in. Thanks for the pull."

He nodded. "Winch comes in mighty handy, this time of year."

"What if *you* get stuck?"

"Have to tie the winch cable around the nearest tree."

"And if there's no tree?"

He shrugged. "Have to get the spare tire out. And bury it . . . fifty feet away. Then attach the winch to *that*."

He had thought of — he had *tried* — everything, in forty-odd years of annual struggles with mud. It had gotten to be a game. But it was no game for me; by the time my wife and I had hiked in our camping gear, each of our four feet was dragging fifteen pounds of clay with it. Veritable Bulgarian peasants. And we had none of the sensible accoutrements — mud boots, bootjacks, mud-room foyers, outdoor decking — that create limits to where mud can turn up and thus prevent it from utterly dominating the quality of life.

We had mud in our tent. We had mud in our sleeping bags, and other private places. By the time May sunshine firmed up our soggy acres, we might have passed for aboriginal mudmen of New Guinea.

One forgets, though. *We* forgot. At the height of summer drought, the same clay soils become as hard as concrete. Vertical cracks open in the good earth that a yardstick cannot plumb. Heavy farm machinery can roll across the landscape and leave not the slightest dent in the topsoil. Seeing all this made it hard to recollect my sunken Porsche.

But mud season never fails, and never disappoints. The very next April, I had my *own* pickup truck — though not a truck equipped with my neighbor's lavish off-road options. On a gray Saturday morning, I ventured forth to buy some high-tensile fence wire from a dealer whose abode lay halfway up a distant mountain. Beyond the pavement's edge. Oh, the road he lived along was surfaced in gravel and maintained by taxpayers; but spring thaw had reduced its driveable width to a single lane of slippery mush, along either side of which oozed dark streams of muck.

I get excited in adverse driving situations. I had a companion with me — also going to buy some fence wire — and he sensed my nervousness as the pickup's rear end fishtailed, rounding a sharp bend. "Sorry," I said. "Think I should slow down?"

"Hell, no. Too greasy. You lose speed, you'll lose all traction."

I was pondering this wisdom when the road straightened out and started up the steepest part of our ascent. I gritted my teeth as the engine found the wild pitch, and then we both saw something large that was half-buried in the road up ahead of us. A *car* — a Chevrolet sedan of indeterminate age — was seemingly treading water smack in the right-of-way.

It wasn't difficult to stop my pickup's forward motion. I don't think I even had to tromp my foot down on the brake; once I had lifted it off the accelerator, the truck wallowed to a halt in a scant few feet. And there we were, stuck in the middle of nowhere.

The Chevy's door opened — or did its driver crawl out the

window? — and a young man slogged toward us in a state of mild perplexity. Not in the least excited. Entertained, certainly. From this calm approach to his remarkable situation — and from the six-ounce "pony" beer bottle clutched in his muddy hand — I quickly identified him as a real Vermonter. "Glad you stopped," he said, as though I had had any choice. "Guess I'm some stuck. Not much traffic up here, either."

"*Now* what?"

"Guess we ought to get me out of the road. Then I'll hike to find a tractor."

"How are we going to get you out of the road?"

"Jack," he answered simply. But the jacking maneuver he proceeded to engage us in was completely unlike any I had ever seen before. First, to create a platform, he sunk his spare tire in the mud beneath his rear bumper. Then, setting the jack on that, he raised the vehicle as high as the sturdy tool would permit. Then he directed us to shove against the fender until the entire car fell off the jack sideways. This moved the Chevy's rear end about two feet toward the road's quicksand-like shoulder.

We repeated the entire procedure on the front end of the car; alternating between the front and the rear, we moved his muddy vehicle clear of the right-of-way in four or five more jack-it-up-and-shove-it-off-the-jack cycles. This took a good hour, during which time no more fools arrived. The three of us were caked in mud, head to foot. Grateful, the Chevy's owner gave each of us a pony bottle of beer.

"Now, you want to try and drive past me?" the young man asked. Seriously.

"No way," I said, sunk to my knees in his astonishing ruts. "I am going to back down off this mountain, and come back in June."

"Why? It's only mud, you know."

Only mud; it was as if he was asking what I did for fun! And this is the prevailing attitude toward the vile, revolting stuff that drags down the spirits of those not born to it. Over time, I have replaced outright loathing of mud season with a mildly game approach. Constant challenge. Win some, lose some. But a measure of the distance I still have to go is that some of my neighbors, in recent years, have managed to elevate mud into an *official* sporting event.

It happened first on Mother's Day — or Mudder's Day, as we

now call it — half a dozen years ago. Several dozen off-road aficionados gathered at a farm named, appropriately, Swampy Acres, and staked out a course that they felt would challenge the most mud-oriented vehicle. A backhoe was employed to scoop out several nifty trenches for contestants to jump across; bulldozers were stationed at each of two livestock-watering ponds that the course plowed straight through. The dozers could fish out any Mudders who became impossibly mired.

The "Mud Run" was an instant success — even though only about one entrant in twenty could reach the finish line of the three-quarter-mile course. And for every finisher, there was apt to be a vehicle that could not be driven from the scene of the battle; axle broken, drive shaft dropped, or transmission cooked. But, since course conditions made speeds above twenty-five miles per hour simply unattainable, the contest was inherently safe. And loads of fun to watch.

Within a few years six thousand souls — from babes in arms to octogenarians — were pouring into Swampy Acres on Mudder's Day. The advertising was almost entirely by word-of-mouth. Saddled with mounting responsibilities for running a big show, the Mudders made themselves a nonprofit corporation and began charging nominal admission fees to pay for portable toilets, insurance, and like expenses. And each year increasingly custom-built, custom-equipped vehicles — more than one hundred of them — would show up to spend the day covering themselves in glop.

Spurred on by the improving quality of competition, the Mudders have had to become wonderfully creative in devising new ways to degrade traction. After all, just *finishing* the course is supposed to be a signal honor in the life of a contestant. Recently I let a dedicated Mudder show me around Swampy Acres, and he had big plans in mind. "See that big old pine tree?" he asked, pointing to the hill. "After we run 'em through the first pond this year, we're going to run 'em up past that tree. There's about a foot of dead pine needles on the ground there. We're going to slather the boys' wheels with mud, then plaster them with dry pine needles."

"Sort of tar and feathering," I pointed out.

"You got it. *Then* you'll see some fancy spinning."

I was impressed.

"And then we're going to dig an uphill jump right beyond that."

"What sort of prize will the winner get?" I asked him.

"Trophy."

"That's all?" I shook my head. Just the *tires* for an all-out mud truck would set a competitor back several hundred dollars.

"That, plus he gets the knowledge that he's really proved something. Once and for all."

Sure, I thought, but proved *what?* That with the right machine, Vermont is *not* just like Bulgaria in mud season? That it is possible to dominate the dreadful ooze? Not to be sucked under, not to have one's spirits dragged down by it? That it is, after all, *only mud?*

The sky rumbled overhead, and rain began to drizzle out of slate-gray April clouds. I turned to leave; by Mother's Day, the mud would be abundant. And the proudest men, commanding marvelous conveyances, would jockey in the muck to find out which of them had feet of clay. I knew *I* did — my boots were caked in the sticky, unrelenting stuff. And I think I realized, then, what it is that Mudders prove: they prove which of us is worthy to live beyond the pavement's edge.

• Live Evaluation

Early last May, I had the opportunity to spend five days poking around an abattoir in Baltimore, under the warm auspices of the United States Department of Agriculture. By week's end, the government had taught me deadly accuracy at a vital skill called Live Evaluation: I could eyeball a slaughter lamb shuffling off a livestock truck and estimate, for example, what percentage of its carcass would consist of kidney and pelvic fat. I could distinguish a High Prime leg from one that was merely Average Choice. I could guess a lamb's age to within a month or two, and judge how well it measured up against an ideal conformation.

A slaughterhouse is the ideal place to learn this skill, because in a matter of hours one can compare one's Live Evaluation notes to the evaluee's chilled carcass — the very proof of the pudding. After going through a hundred lambs or so, a person becomes adept at what amounts to X-ray vision. If beauty, in an animal, is more than skin-deep, one's powers of appraisal can be made equal to the challenge of discerning it.

I was sure that, as a shepherd, I would have occasion to put this valuable training to good use; whenever buyers and sellers of lamb converse, the language of Live Evaluation is employed to characterize the quality of what is being marketed. But I had no idea that my newly acquired skill would come in handy on the very day I returned home to Vermont. It was a Saturday; my wife informed me that the Miss Vermont Pageant was being held that very evening, and that we were going.

Now, I was aware that a Miss Vermont pageant existed — *someone* had to represent the state in Atlantic City — and that in recent years the pageant had been held in nearby Middlebury. I knew these things because a couple of years ago I had wandered into a bar in Middlebury late on a Saturday night, and sitting on a tall stool was a young woman with a banner draped across her chest. MISS VERMONT, the banner said. On the bar, next to the woman's glass, was a little crown. "Hey, I won!" she called to well-wishers across the room. That's life in the sticks, I thought — first you get crowned Miss Vermont and then you slip away to hoist a few beers at the local pub. Just folks, see?

But little did I realize that the Miss Vermont Pageant would be, at its most basic level, a Live Evaluation extravaganza. The pasted-on smiles, the mannequin-like figures, and the cookie-cutter sameness among contestants that I thought typified beauty pageants have no place in Vermont; leafing through the program, I saw that photographs of each of the sixteen hopefuls plainly depicted a Rugged Individual. An unfortunate corollary, revealed in a chart of historical interest, was that not once in sixty-two years had a Miss Vermont managed to be crowned Miss America.

The house lights, in the Middlebury Union High School auditorium, dimmed all at once, and an audience of roughly four hundred connoisseurs of beauty came to rapt attention. The tape-recorded theme from the Broadway show *Dream Girls* began to play, and suddenly eager girls were strutting all across the stage — girls with catchy names like Miss Bellows Falls, Miss Rutland, Miss Essex Junction. Trouble was, to my trained eye the typical contestant was something less than a Dream Girl. Some even raised difficult questions about the pageant's recruiting system.

But the Dream Girls walk-on was just to get the evening started, and the contestants soon disappeared offstage. Then, in quick succession, we were introduced to the reigning Miss Vermont, the reigning Miss New Hampshire, and the reigning Miss Massachusetts. Neither of the other two states had ever won a Miss America contest, either. Alluding to this, the emcee noted that a single gown in Miss Texas' wardrobe for Atlantic City was likely to cost more than the Miss Vermont Pageant's entire budget. No wonder our girls seemed to lack the self-confidence, the panache, the style that make for a winner.

I was pondering these dismal truths when who should step onstage but the reigning Miss America herself. From a far-off state where winter does not exist. Everybody rose up in a thunderous ovation, as though our shabby rural lives had just been touched by magic; in her slinky sequined dress, Miss America proceeded to belt out a couple of songs. Then she recounted some of the wonderful experiences of her reign, such as meeting Ronald Reagan. Such as getting to be a team captain on TV's "Family Feud." Neither of these goals seemed particularly worth aspiring to, but who was I to judge? When it came to appraising things, my specialty was Live Evaluation; I gave Miss America a High Prime leg score, Average Prime overall conformation, and a Yield Grade score of 2 — an excellent ratio of lean meat to fat and bone. Based on everything I had learned in Baltimore, this lovely creature would certainly have pleased a packer.

Then, having established this remarkably high standard, Miss America left us and the Miss Vermont contestants were paraded in — wearing swimsuits. "Well?" my wife asked, nudging me. "What do you think?"

"Average Good to Low Choice, mainly, with some wastiness about the thigh and an Average Yield Grade of 4," I replied.

"Get out of here!"

"Hey, wait. I *know* this. Beauty's more than skin-deep, right?"

"You are awful."

"Isn't this a beauty contest?"

"Think of it as a *talent* show. Fifty percent of the points are for talent."

"Right," I said. "And men read *Playboy* for all those thoughtful articles, too."

"These girls are competing for scholarship money. To further their educations. No shame in that."

Indeed, scholarships were to be awarded; why, the two Preliminary Swimsuit Award winners were each going to get twenty-five dollars from an Anonymous Donor. Enough money to buy about half a swimsuit. There were three other small-change awards. The winner, though, was in for roughly four thousand dollars in scholarship money and one thousand dollars' worth of clothes. The biggest contributor to this kitty was a local silo company, rumored to be nearly bankrupt. Not your typical commercial sponsor. Would the next Miss Vermont be able to collect? Would she have to pose atop a silo?

"No," I whispered to my wife as the swimsuit contest ended. "I just can't believe these nice girls entered this thing for the money. They have bought the dream. The mythos: '*There she goes* . . . .' Every man's ideal. That's what they'd all like to prove about themselves."

"I like that Miss West Rupert, there."

"Barely make it into the Choice grade."

"Look at how she moves, see?"

I watched her long legs stalk offstage. "What this whole thing shows is, men can still get women to do just about anything. Give these girls a hoop, and they'll line right up to jump through it. It's as though the last fifteen years had never happened."

"Sssh, someone's going to hear you."

"Women must be the most insecure creatures — just think about fashion and cosmetics and hairdos. Women are sheep. There's probably nothing you couldn't get a woman to . . . "

"Women don't fight wars," my wife said.

"So?"

"So that's where *men* are sheep. And, look, this contest isn't hurting anyone. So just shut up."

I did shut up — all the way through the Talent Competition, in which one contestant in a black lamé jumpsuit played the flute, another twirled colorful flags while performing a gymnastic routine, and a third did a nifty tap dance. Most, though, had a song to sing or a dramatic monologue to recite — usually about a lost or estranged lover, and always well beyond the performer's rather limited emotional range.

The talent show was followed by an intermission — "halftime," as the man behind me called it. Just like in football. But I stayed rooted to my seat, afraid of meeting someone I might know and being asked my opinion of the pageant. When the house lights went down again, we were greeted by a live and positively jolting drumroll. A young man offstage barked out a military command, and suddenly the Norwich University Regimental Drill Team was marching down the aisles and swarming across the stage. Of all things! A little army to represent masculine neuroses in this festival of feminine neuroses. The marchers jiggled their guns around and stomped on the floor a bit; they drew their ceremonial swords and sheathed them several times; and then, to heartfelt applause, they paraded out of the auditorium.

"Now, who the hell's idea was *that?*" I asked my wife.

"Probably the same folks who — what was I saying? About men? And wars?"

The military entertainment was a prelude to the Miss Vermont Evening Gown Competition, in which each finalist was introduced and actually said a few words to let us know a little about herself. With waiting-room Muzak schmaltzing up the background, one girl after another explained why winning this contest was important to her — not that it all hadn't been a whale of a lot of fun, but this was down-to-business time.

"Have you picked the winner yet?"

"There's only one who'll go High Choice," I said. "Miss Middlebury College. The Yield Grade is 1, the leg is Low Prime. Conformation could be better, but it says right in the regulations: 'Superior quality can compensate for deficient conformation, on an equal basis.'"

"Yes, and you can go straight back to Baltimore."

The judges, the real ones, pondered their decision while we once again met Miss Massachusetts, and heard another song from Miss America, and bid farewell to last year's Miss Vermont. And then the *Dream Girls* theme came up, followed by the Dream Girls themselves, followed by the Norwich University Regimental Drill Team. Raising their polished swords to make an arch of flashing steel, these uniformed and priapic young men stood bug-eyed as Miss America sashayed through to announce the winner. And the winner was . . .

"Miss Middlebury College!"

"See!" I crowed, rising to my feet with the cheering crowd. "What did I say? High Choice!"

"She isn't even from Vermont, I hear," sniffed my wife.

"That doesn't matter, these days. Got to send the very best we can to Atlantic City. California, Texas, Mississippi; somehow those

states grow 'em out better than we can up here. Miss Vermont is —
it's almost like sending a lamb to slaughter."

• Literary Culture

For the first couple of months of my tenure in Vermont, when
people asked me what I did I answered without trace of shame or
embarrassment that I was a novelist. That I wrote fiction. This self-
characterization — buttressed incontrovertibly by published
works — had successfully awed and interested strangers in my
former life, and I felt certain it would raise the esteem in which my
new neighbors held me.

I was mistaken, though. A person up here *does* something like
milk cows, run a backhoe, cut timber, drive a truck. A person does
not *do* something like write fiction. Perhaps, in the whole wide
world, there might be a dozen scriveners churning out novels to
fill the supermarket racks, but such an occupation could scarcely
be considered work. And the chances of one of those literati being
me — living in a tent pitched in the pasture of the Donaldson place
— was virtually nil. And what's more, if I *was* somehow a novelist,
why, it meant that I was aiding and abetting and cashing in on the
sorry breakdown of traditional society, the erosion of morality and
decency.

How did such a message get communicated? Very simply. It
started with the loaded question: "What do you write books
about?"

"About? Well, I — just any issues that concern me."

"Hmnh! You ever try to write a best-seller?"

"Well, sure, I've *tried*, but . . . "

"I know how to write a best-seller. Put sex in it. Put a *lot* of sex
in it; that works, every time. Right?"

"Gee," I used to answer disingenuously. "I never thought of
that, exactly." Fact is, I *had* written about sex, but I had a bad habit
of failing to write about sex in a way that made folks want to go
out and try it. Perhaps my neighbors saw things clearly; perhaps
that is why best-sellers had eluded me. I was suddenly grateful,
though, grateful that these real Vermonters could not easily lay
hands on what I had published before trying to join their ranks. I
had enough explaining to do already.

In time, I felt that I had to become something more than a novelist in my neighbors' eyes — and in my own eyes, too — if I wanted to fit in. So I became, in rough order, a homesteader, owner-builder, carpenter, and sheep farmer; each new identity helped me get a little further off the hook, until nowadays most folks consider me practically normal. Deep in my breast, though, lurks a gagged novelist itching to jeopardize my hard-won status as a solid citizen.

There are many Vermonters, on the other hand, who care deeply about writers and writing, and who strive to leaven rural lives with the yeast of literary culture. I first met some of these types by attending a meeting of the League of Vermont Writers. Far from the exclusive clique of intellectuals that I had expected, this league proved to be completely undiscriminating. *Anyone* could join, and the actual *writers* were more apt to apply their talents to church newsletters or small-town gossip sheets than to anything so strenuous as a book-length narrative. Still, writing was their bag.

The League of Vermont Writers meets several times each year, typically to hear a program comprising one recently published children's book author; one publisher from a small, obscure publishing house; and one editor from a regional magazine. Now and then an actual novelist comes to speak, leaving everybody green with envy and convinced, once again, that what sells books today is sex. And more sex. That's why it is so hard for a *good* — an unsexed — author to succeed in getting published.

I joined the League of Vermont Writers — why not? — but doing so did not resolve my identity crisis; I still sensed a terrible contradiction between trying to be a writer and becoming a Vermonter. But membership did thrust me into the company of people for whom reading books was not a suspicious pastime. One of these persons — an attractive, thoughtful older woman — suggested that I accompany her to the book-discussion club at her local public library.

"Book-discussion club? Here?"

"You'd just love it! We could use a few more men, too. Tuesday nights, we meet, and you can pick up a copy of whatever book we're reading at the library desk. Free; it's all free, you know. Then some professor comes to talk about the book to us, and we all discuss it. Just like going to college, don't you know?"

So I accompanied the woman to a discussion on Arthur Miller's drama *The Crucible*, the most extraordinary book discussion I have ever taken part in. What, the professor mused, was the connection between adolescent girls in a Puritan society and the medieval conception of witches?

"Guy just probably wanted to try to get some sex into it," some book lover answered. "So's it would sell, I suppose."

What lessons, the leader wondered, might be drawn for the present era concerning the stigmatization and persecution of those who seem different from the rest of us?

"Have to make them stop it somehow, 'cause we don't have the capital punishment anymore today."

Were there any questions from the audience? the frustrated teacher asked.

A trio of women in the back row stirred, and one asked: "Well, what do you think about those witches up there on Mount Philo?"

"Uh, I beg your pardon?"

"Every Sunday night they're up there. Everybody knows about it. Singing those chants, and hexing people. I hear they put the evil eye on old Maurice LaFountain — well, what do *you* think?"

This, I thought, was *not* just like a literature class in college. And it was too real for me. I sloped out quietly, leaving the professor in a patient effort to explain that, although the local papers had advertised this evening as a discussion of alleged witchcraft in colonial Salem, it was not precisely meant to be a discussion of witchcraft. How the crowd received this news, I am not sure; but I left that evening ready to eschew the local element that professes to be concerned with letters.

In fact, as time went by I came to adopt my neighbors' wise perspective that somebody who calls himself a novelist is probably a questionable character. As a rule, I now avoid the company of novelists; and for myself, I strive never to project a literary persona.

We have, though, in this broad valley on the shores of Lake Champlain, several renowned institutions of higher learning. In the ordinary course of events, these schools can be counted on to import a few famous writers now and again — novelists and poets sufficiently acclaimed to be above suspicion. Often they give public readings. And sometimes, when these *hommes de lettres* approach celebrity status, when they are *Time* magazine cover material, even I cannot resist the opportunity to go hear — no, *smell* — them.

So it was that last winter I ventured across the snowy landscape to attend a fiction reading from a work-in-progress, a writer's highbrow term for something unfinished. The novelist in question was accomplished, hugely successful, and *hot*; but even so, I did not think it necessary to arrive more than twenty minutes before the appointed hour to insure getting a seat. In fact, when I reached the hall I found it so deserted that I ran out to pick up some groceries at the nearest store, which turned out to be an organic foods cooperative. On a table by the cash register, I saw what appeared to be a New Left tabloid; curious, I bought a copy. Then back to the lecture hall, seating capacity four hundred, where this time I noticed a small card taped to the door:

DUE TO ANTICIPATED AUDIENCE, THIS AFTERNOON'S
READING HAS BEEN MOVED TO PAINTER AUDITORIUM

Very well; Painter Auditorium could seat six hundred, and it was but a few minutes' walk away. Arriving there, *still* before the stated hour, I was astonished to see several hundred people shuffling about in the snow outside the building. Most were college students in their brightly colored ski parkas, but there was a generous smattering of League of Vermont Writers and book-discussion-club types, too. I saw the woman who had taken me to discuss *The Crucible*, and greeted her. "Haven't they opened up yet?" I asked.

"Full! That hall's full up!"

"To hear a novelist?" I shook my head. "Well, if it's full up, why don't we all go home?"

"Because they might move the reading again. To the gymnasium. That's what everybody's waiting to see."

"How many can the gymnasium hold?"

"Oh, about a thousand."

All of a sudden, the doors to Painter Auditorium burst open and its six hundred occupants poured out as though there were a bomb inside. They sprinted off across the snow in the direction of the gym — a good quarter mile away, and uphill to boot — and most of the milling crowd outside joined the wild stampede.

"Bonnie!" shrieked a coed on crutches to a friend who was

apparently out for track. "Save me a seat — please! I want to see that man!"

The crowd surged past us, but my elderly acquaintance scoffed and headed for her car. "I've never had to run to hear a novelist yet," she said. "And I'm not starting now. No matter *who* he is."

I nearly succumbed to these sentiments. A novelist is not, after all, Mick Jagger. And yet, and yet — we don't get such stars here every day of the week. I took a step, then started to jog half-heartedly; suddenly I was racing like all the rest of them, jostling for position on the icy slope.

I got a seat — and not everyone did, even in that large hall with its bleachers and expanse of floor. I looked around, breathless, and everywhere were beautiful young women come to hear this author. Countless gallons of shampoo had been lavished on the event, and a great deal of thought spent on tastefully seductive dress. Amazing. And I, waiting for the great man to appear, pulled out my tabloid from the organic foods co-op.

It turned out to be a lesbian newspaper. Sexually explicit, too. I felt my cheeks color, and I felt the coeds all around me shifting in their hard seats to put some space between themselves and the strange fellow perusing smut at a literary gathering.

And then the novelist strode in, to an ovation such as a saint might hope to get. After an obsequious and lengthy introduction, he was given the podium and allowed to read. About what? Gonorrhea, prostitution, butcher-block abortion: sex, sex, and more sex. The beautiful young women smiled beatifically, visibly moved by the transcendent power of literature.

I listened as long as I could, then pocketed my lesbian rag and tiptoed to the door. The thing about being a novelist is: to win is to be canonized, to lose is to be made a pariah. In rural Vermont, at least. Oh, the squelched novelist inside me screamed: "Idiot! Doesn't that look like fun!" But I told my inner self that literary culture in a place like this is not to be confused — not at any cost — with literature.

• Buying Used

In rural New England, the shopping impulse so characteristic of Americans is very substantially muted. Shopping malls, those modern temples, are nearly nonexistent; many towns would feel privileged to be able to support a simple five-and-dime. Recreational shopping, as practiced in the suburbs, is not the style in my quiet corner of Vermont. We lack opportunities, and we also lack the bucks — another example of the chicken-and-egg problem.

What is particularly telling about my neighbors' attitudes toward acquisition is that "buying *new*" constitutes an eccentric subcategory of the art of purchasing. "Buying *new*" is reserved for vain, or flagrantly well-heeled, or wildly hasty shoppers; far more sensible is to locate merchandise that has been owned once before. Or *several* times before. The more owners that a chair or sink or skillet may have served, why, the more convincing its pedigree. And the less one usually has to pay to obtain it.

Merchandising any item requires a measure of overhead expense; second-hand selling, though, cuts this to the bone. An extreme — and extremely popular — example is the lawn sale, in which price tags are affixed to sundry household trash. Then, on some sunny afternoon in midsummer, the items for sale are prominently set out along the public thoroughfare. Labor aside, a lawn sale's chief expense is the production of a few cardboard signs with arrows.

The lawn sale mystique requires that such signs be as crude as possible; believe it or not, though, there are people who cruise the backroads of my county with their eyes peeled for them. Some may be connoisseurs of true Americana — the jelly jar designed for serving pudding when the jelly's gone, the N.F.L. team whiskey glasses that you used to get each time you bought a full tank of gas — but most lawn sale devotees are, in their own way, shopping. This is an appropriate means of obtaining housewares.

Lawn sales are strictly a fair-weather sport; when showers threaten, all the ratty card tables of bric-a-brac have to be hustled under cover. I credit the pressures of our fickle climate, therefore, with a proliferation of garage sales. Garage sales are lawn sales moved into the nearest garage — low rent, see? But once established, garage sales can be sustained all summer long. When inventory levels suffer, neighbors are only too happy to replenish the stock in return for minding the store. The cardboard signs announce: GIGANTIC SEVEN-FAMILY GARAGE SALE JUST ONE MILE BEAR LEFT! Such a sale might be just the place to furnish an old house or equip a kitchen.

Lawn sales and garage sales cannot offer ultimate bargains to the wily shopper, however much they undercut retail prices. The reason is that, like a store, the lawn sale offers goods for sale at a certain suggested price over a reasonable length of time. In sharp contrast, auctions offer goods for sale at no particular price — or at a price to be determined by the shoppers themselves — and for a very brief instant in time. This makes auction sales hugely popular with cunning buyers; but the seller has a compensating incentive, too. He may not love the price, but at auction the seller knows his merchandise will absolutely be sold.

Auctions make for entertaining drama as well as bargains. In the most common variety of summer auction, somebody has died and his estate is being settled; the auction converts all worldly possessions, no matter how precious or mundane, into coin of the realm. Weepy kin are apt to be dispersed among the crowd, watching memories sold to disrespectful strangers, but the general atmosphere is apt to be celebratory. A carnival: hot dog vendors, cars parked on the grass, cheerful citizens sitting in lawn chairs facing the front porch. In the house, a squad of muscled teenagers wrestles stuff out the door in no particular order. Kitchen range, rocking chair, pickling crock, mattress, chain saw. Each is duly made the property of the highest bidder; when the contents of the house are sold, sometimes they sell the *house*. By day's end, one person's life's possessions have been divvied up and redistributed as swiftly as a stolen sports car in some urban chop shop.

In a good estate auction, the deceased may make his or her presence felt; when a local *grande dame* died at the age of 110, half the town of Middlebury turned out for an auction that was a cathartic expression of community affection. But in another common type of rural auction, there is no deceased but only an all-too-living bankrupt bailing out of some financial misadventure. Usually it is a farm. Farm dispersal auctions draw an audience from far and wide, and one need not be a farmer to enjoy them at the level of richly human theater. It's important to remember that farm auction attendance is always in inverse proportion to how fine the weather is. If the sun is shining, chances are the turnout will be small; but rainy days that hamper field work result in startling auction crowds of amiable vultures come to pick apart a lost farm's corpse.

Modern farms tend to be spread-out affairs, and the auctioneer must lead his herd of bidders from barn to machinery shed to milkhouse, chanting into a portable public-address system as he goes. Since much of the value on a farm is in machinery — and since machinery must be maintained to function properly — the farmer who is selling out usually assumes the job of mounting every tractor and demonstrating that it starts, or running a manure loader through its hydraulic paces, or spinning a hay rake's tines to show how smooth the bearings are. When a tractor coughs to life, no matter with what difficulty, the auctioneer crows: "There it is, boys! All in working order!" It is an exaggerated claim, but everybody *knows* that. Machinery at auction is lucky to bring thirty-five cents on the dollar.

A good farm auction, too, is packed with representatives of various financial interests. Bankers. Farm lending agents. Dealers of machinery, who sell their wares on company-financed credit just like Ford or General Motors. And there may be loan sharks present, ready to do business with particular farmers on particularly attractive items. This can lead to two-step bidding, when a farmer has to search a lender's face across the crowd for the faintest nod that gives permission to stay in the game.

Cosmetics play a well-respected part in the farm auction ritual, notwithstanding that almost nobody is fooled. It's just the way one *does* things. Cows are gussied up and perhaps not fully milked, to create the impression of having whopping udders. Grease and dirt are steam-cleaned from late-model machinery, and often the new spray paint on some rusted hunk of iron is still dripping wet. The effort is the thing, the same sort of effort one would hire in a good mortician. One expects new paint, and one expects corrosion right beneath it; what is unexpected, though — and cannot be faked, nor fail to impress even the casual observer — is the utter stoicism with which a farm family can watch the dismemberment of what they have spent a lifetime lovingly creating. Visitors who scarcely know a teat from a toenail leave such auctions deeply moved.

The third and most accessible variety of rural auction is founded on what passes, in the hinterlands, for paying protection money to one public-spirited drinking society or another. Does the volunteer fire department need a new hose? Do the Lions want to buy a chest X-ray machine? Does a school-parents group want to fund a scholarship? Very well, the answer is a Benefit Auction.

Susceptible parties are hit up to donate auction items, and a crowd is rustled up to bid for them some summer evening on the town green. There may be a barbecue. An ice-cream stand. A flea market. With a tremendous expenditure in human effort, relatively meager sums of money can be reliably raised.

At the first such benefit auction that my wife and I attended in Vermont, we purchased two refrigerators. Five dollars apiece, and all in working order — which is to say that, when plugged in, something would whir inside. The pair of them averaged thirty years old. I planned to set one up for brewing lager beer; my wife wanted to cold-smoke hams in the other. Little did we know that the thirty-year-old, five-dollar refrigerator is an absolutely classic benefit auction item. Homely, noisy, smelly, frosty — we never did *anything* with these terrific bargains. After they occupied space for two or three years, we donated them to another benefit auction. More advanced societies use landfills to retire such items.

Businesses make easy marks for coughing up benefit auction merchandise, and they lend a modicum of class to such events by having a few new goods to sell amongst the old. New, although probably overstocked or returned or dead on the shelves. I think, though — based on recent offerings at benefit auctions — that the entrepreneurial class is getting tired of having to shell out protection money to one outfit after another. There seems to be an effort underway to poke fun at these sales, as when a local dress shop donated some of the more risqué undergarments one might expect to find in Vermont to a recent Lions Club Benefit Auction

"Well, well," said the auctioneer, a man not hired to find himself at a loss for words. He dangled the merchandise at arm's length like some dead mouse found beneath the cupboard. *"These* should liven things up after evening chores. Come on, ladies! Who'll give ten dollars on these, uh, these . . ."

"Lingerie," his sidekick told him.

"Lingerie. Right."

The ladies, for reasons best known to them, refused to bid. In time, though, a couple of men did, and the crowd enjoyed a good laugh. Fifteen minutes later, the old auctioneer was caught in a worse embarrassment. A local surgeon, he read off a card, was donating a simple, minor *operation* to the benefit auction. To the highest bidder. Now he faltered: "Vast . . . Vas . . . "

"Vasectomy," his sidekick whispered.

"Vasectomy! Right! Now, what fella's going to bid on that? Make you real popular! Start the bidding at one hunnerd fifty dollars, and all for a good cause, too."

Just in front of where I sat, a Vermonter asked his wife: "Whuzuhell's vast-ectomy?"

"Think I might have read about that in a ladies' magazine," she said.

"Hey! Hey! Let's go! How much am I bid?"

For reasons best known to themselves, not one man placed a bid. In time, though, several *women* did, presumably in behalf of someone else who may or may not have read a ladies' magazine, or known what was being auctioned. In the end, though, no one felt this operation worth the reserve price that its donor had placed on it. With a sigh of relief, the auctioneer returned to hustling thirty-year-old refrigerators and tired, dirty mattresses and broken lawn mowers. *Used* goods. Cheap. Bargains.

Recreational shopping? Up here, we don't practice it the same way as folks do in cities. But honest merchandise does tend to get bought and sold — and bought and sold, and bought again. And, by golly, sometimes we do have fun at it.

• Cheap Thrills

I have an acquaintance who collects a full year's social debts, then pays them off by hosting a wild evening of capture the flag in his steep and rock-strewn woodlot. It is, to my mind, a quintessential Vermont bash. Active. Daring. Held in a unique and gorgeous outdoor setting. And, by any calculus of offbeat grown-up entertainment, it ranks as a night of unmitigated fun.

As is common in these parts, my friend moves in social circles that cut across convenient lines of class, education, and sociology; he invites, I now suspect, everybody that he knows. Up to one hundred souls will troop out to the forest clearing where he parks his jeep — laden with finger food and kegs of beer and elaborate first aid supplies — just as a summer's afternoon fades into evening. There will be a B.Y.O. meat barbecue, which will metamorphose after dark into a bonfire. After a sufficient happy hour, sides are chosen for the big event.

Capture the flag is a war game, it will be recalled. In the

woodlot where we play, each army is assigned a five-acre kingdom; these border on, and are buffered by, a neutral zone where the food and drink and fire offer respite for the weary soldier. Before the game begins, each side scouts its home premises; a jail is located for detaining captured enemies, and a flag — a *large* flag — is unfurled in some offbeat place where it will defy easy apprehension. Scouts and spies, defensive guards and jailors are all designated. And then, at a blast from the jeep's horn, the game begins.

The game can go on for hours — until after dark, sometimes. The game is not won until one side discovers its opponent's flag, manages to heist it, and runs it back across the boundary to the neutral zone. This would not be a formidable task, except that players tagged by their opponents on foreign soil must submit to being escorted to jail. There they languish, crouched behind some rude stump or boulder, to be released only if a fearless comrade dodges guards and spies and jailors and succeeds in tagging the prisoners free.

Generally, I spend a good portion of this annual soirée holed up in jail. Incarceration does not, however, remove a player from the field of conflict. An important ground rule requires that jailors provide beer for their charges. Ad libitum — which means endless trips to the beer truck in the clearing. Thirsty detainees, demanding their rights constantly, can force their opponents to commit an unwise proportion of their army to jail duty; this can have strategic implications. On the other hand, one year my entire team wound up drunk in jail — all at the same time — and so we lost the battle by default.

Warfare must have been a ball, in some distant past. I understand that the Green Mountain Boys enjoyed it. War is a magnificent leveler, too; I have seen half-literate farmhands mapping strategy with full professors of neuroanatomy. Farriers tackling lawyers, and vice versa. I have witnessed circumspect, mild-mannered men and women whooping like savages, darting from behind one broad tree trunk to the next, and dancing over positively treacherous terrain in dim, uncertain light. My friend the host is a young physician; last year, he sent two of his guests to the local emergency room to have injuries checked. Both managed to mend just fine. Both are looking forward to the next capture the flag party.

This, in the rural boonies far north and west of Boston, is our idea of entertainment. Part of it, at any rate.

There was a time in my life when I placed a premium on having access to sophisticated cultural pleasures. Most often, this meant witnessing performances — theater and music, poetry and dance — or attending art exhibitions at grand museums. I did not, in moving to Vermont, plan on swearing off this feast of human creativity that I enjoyed. Vermont is not, say, North Dakota; and the farm I purchased was reasonably proximate to regional centers of higher learning. Montreal was just a two-hour drive away. Even New York was but a couple of hundred miles south. I felt sure that when I wanted formal entertainment, I could go find it without unreasonable inconvenience.

Something about rural life, though, turns a person inward. The cultivation of self-reliance — necessary to successful living in this beautiful but cruelly demanding landscape — gradually extended itself from fundamental skills like keeping warm, like keeping fed, into the realm of diversion and relaxation. I found I no longer relished being a spectator of culture; I sought entertainments that were more active and involving and immediate.

Then, too, I suspected soon enough that the offerings of high culture in places like Vermont were mere crumbs dropped from some distant, overburdened table. Stale crumbs, at times; or acts deemed not yet ready for discerning, urban audiences.

Then, too, I discovered that on any given evening, the range of choice of cultural offerings in Vermont is so narrow as to be demeaning. I had valued casting what I perceived as cultural votes — what to attend, what to spurn — but the fact of rural life was that far too often I found only one name on the ballot.

Nowadays, I rarely venture forth to enjoy the arts — though artists manage to trek up this way relentlessly, under various auspices. Yet I have not totally excused myself from the cultural banquet; rather, I have found ways to approach it at my own unpolished level. This, I find, is much to be preferred.

The best and longest-running party I have been to in Vermont was a local Shakespeare circle: me, my wife, a journeyman carpenter, a day-care worker, a puppeteer, and a teacher of French literature. For two winters, we met nearly every Sunday to eat and drink and read aloud whichever of the bard's plays struck our fancy. Eventually we completed the entire canon.

In a city, I imagine such an approach to Shakespeare would founder, stillborn, on the shoals of self-consciousness. Read-alouds are amateurish, unstaged, unlikely to inspire; but in a rural and wintry place where there is no competition — where there is, quite frankly, damn little else to do — certain features of such readings stand out and commend themselves. In a group of six, each reader has to manage several parts; one becomes involved with the dramatis personae far more intimately than one would in either silent reading or by attendance at live performances, however masterful. One can read the lesser and rarely staged plays, as well as the favorites. One need not abridge a single scene. The histories can be read as a cumulative block of drama, as a chronology. Who can see them staged this way?

But most of all, I recall the splendid informality of our Sunday Shakespeare readings. If I failed to understand an idiom, a line or two — if I lost the track completely — I was not condemned to sitting hopelessly confused, as at a performance. I could say: "Now, hold it — what the hell is going on?" I could pause to stretch, to sip hot tea or wine or something stronger; among my thoughtful but completely unpedantic friends, we could discuss the play even as it was unfolding.

Over time, we found the perfect structure for such readings. We would gather at one of our homes in mid-afternoon, each person bringing a *Collected Works* and an assigned portion of our dinner. Over tea — and after a cross-country ski, often enough — we would choose that Sunday's play. After reading two acts, we would stop to sup. Then, in a marvelous glow of rich desserts and coffee and liqueurs, we would polish off the drama. Could there be a finer, a more civilized way to enjoy a cold night in Vermont? And the price of admission was merely the hands-on attitude toward cultural entertainment that becomes a survival skill in such a rural place.

A final thrill, while never precisely cheap but seldom as expensive as one might expect, is to dine with utter distinction on completely local fare. In a country where so many live on Pepsi and potato chips, this worthy goal can become a sociable obsession. And among those so obsessed, including individuals of only modest means and completely unexclusive tastes, the level of culinary skills can run very high. Also, our cooks often have ingredients to work with of impeccable quality: absolutely fresh, pure food untainted by preservatives or chemicals. Buying cream, one can specify that it be from a Jersey cow. Buying lamb, one can specify a loin or leg that was finished on whole barley. Buying honey, one can specify one's favorite blossom: apple, clover, trefoil, alfalfa.

Friends of ours — he is a welder, she a quiltmaker — know what they consider to be a good time in Vermont. They like hiking to some remote and lovely spot, then spreading out a superb picnic. Nothing unfit for a king, and atop a mountain, nibbling salmon mousse, who could resist feeling royal?

Once my wife and I enjoyed an outing with these closet gourmands; I recall we had to bring champagne. Our destination was a mountaintop pond on the Long Trail, several miles from Middlebury Gap. But it had been a wet summer, and the footpath was at turns extremely slippery or impossibly muddy. After half an hour's frustration, we turned round and drove back to the broad, lush, manicured lawn that surrounds the Bread Loaf campus of Middlebury College, halfway up the mountain. This seemed a fitting spot for our epicurean repast; we carried our hampers fifty yards in from the road and spread a linen tablecloth.

No sooner had we unpacked, than I saw a groundskeeper stalking toward us from the buildings in the distance. "Here comes the law," I said.

My friend popped a champagne cork and filled our crystal goblets. "Eat," he said. "Look elegant."

Looking elegant is not our natural style, but we did our very best. By the time the groundskeeper reached us, we were enjoying fresh rainbow trout and broccoli with hollandaise — and much else — while perching delicate china plates in our laps.

"Private property," he hollered, "you can't . . . " But then he saw this was no ordinary picnic. He stared. He shook his head. "Just this once," he said. "That's some picnic, that is."

And indeed it was. Could one enjoy such a meal in refined, urban, civilized environments? Absolutely; right off some distinguished restaurant's menu, like as not. But could one enjoy it half so thoroughly as we did, on that gentle summer's eve? Not on my aspic. Thrown back on our own resources as we simple country folk are, every taste of civilized, sophisticated pleasure packs a special sweetness. It's a seasoning that I am not sure I could locate, elsewhere.

CHAPTER TWO

The Compleat Shepherd

*T*HE RE-EMERGENCE, OVER THE past decade or so, of a commercial sheep industry in northern New England was completely unforeseen, even by specialists in the field of agricultural development. Sheep had grazed here by the millions in the nineteenth century, but with the opening of western ranges and the creation of cross-continental transportation systems, sheep production costs in New England became uncompetitively high. Dairy farming came into fashion, and the rest is history: in Vermont today, ninety percent of agricultural receipts go to the dairy industry.

Conventional wisdom, just a few years ago, held that sheep could not be profitable in a farm economy characterized by scarce and expensive open land, a prejudice for capital-intensive production methods, and the virtual absence of any agricultural services oriented to the needs of would-be shepherds. Sheep, for example, need shearers — and there were not many. There were no specialized feeds, few health supplies, and relatively few veterinarians skilled with sheep. There were no slaughterhouses killing lambs efficiently enough for interstate wholesale trade, and no terminal markets or even livestock auction houses trading in lamb at national market prices. There was next to nothing on which to predicate an industry.

Into this environment waltzed the urban refugees and back-to-the-landers of the early 1970s. They were people somewhat like myself: overeducated, somewhat underfinanced ideologues, people far more likely to hold college degrees in modern dance or art history than in agricultural science. They came looking for a simple life, and to find it they were prepared to become vastly less productive citizens than society had encouraged them to be.

I do not suggest these pilgrims came upcountry to raise sheep; they came to grow vegetables, most likely, or fruits and berries. Self-sufficiency was the oft-reiterated goal, a mantra placing the newcomers squarely in Thoreau's footsteps. There was little emphasis on growing food for marts of trade. Yet many of those who tried to make the soil yield vegetables couldn't help noticing that Vermont soils prefer to yield grass. Forage crops: timothy and clover, bluegrass, redtop, trefoil, brome. People cannot eat these crops except as they are mediated for our benefit by ruminant animals. The ones that have four stomachs. So people much like myself — people who liked to mix their own granola, people prone to dabbling in vegetarianism — came to see that livestock play a critical role in wise and sustainable farming systems.

Some bought beef cows, some bought goats. But sheep, God bless them, had personality traits and cultural connotations that made them profoundly appealing to the refugees. A marriage made in heaven: sheep were meek and mild, pacific — or defenseless, at any rate — and shepherding could place a person in a rich tradition dating back to the Old Testament, not to mention Jesus Christ. In the iconography of that counterculture, who on earth would choose to be a cowboy rather than a shepherd?

Getting any agricultural development off the ground takes a tremendous amount of critical mass; in the case of bringing sheep back to New England, the cadre of early-retired hippies swelled the depleted ranks of small-time sheep producers enormously. But, as anybody knows, just a few sheep will lose a lot of money for their shepherd, no matter how earnest. Flocks got bigger; *more* money was lost, but marginal production costs were lowered to tantalizing levels. With a few *more* sheep . . .

The new shepherds were nothing if not stubborn. They were

educable, too; in fact, many of them had no real skills apart from being expert students. Some were inventors, some were keen geneticists, some brought training in creating economic models. All, however, were to some degree square pegs that had not fit smoothly into the round holes of society. Few at first were prone to cooperate for some dimly perceived mutual benefit, but, over time, those who stuck with sheep developed their own flocking instinct, too.

My farm turned the corner a couple of years ago; with just about one hundred sheep, the numbers changed from red to black. Some folks needed more sheep to achieve the same exciting feat; others needed fewer. But nowadays, people actually move here to become sheep farmers. And other people — ag experts — can show them a variety of ways to be successful at it. As well as many ways to fail.

Around Vermont today, grazing sheep are a perfectly common sight. No one even slows his car to gawk. It *is* a marvel, though. And when I think of all the inappropriate talents, the varieties of ignorance, and the wealth of misinformation that *I* brought to shepherding — why, I am filled with laughter and amazement. Imagine people like me helping to create a new agricultural industry! I shake my head and say: this is the most unlikely, and the most interesting, thing that I have ever done.

• Fertility Rites

I began characterizing myself as a farmer a couple of years before I was farming much of anything; I had, after all, moved to Vermont. Wasn't that enough? My old urban friends were credulous types, and besides, I *could* tell a plow from a harrow. But in fact I was no farmer. It was a tentative, almost wistful self-description. I happened to have bought a farm, but I didn't have the vaguest notion what to do with it.

Local folks would ask me what kind of farming I planned to get into, and I had a splendid answer. I would say: "Organic!" I was going to be a friend of the earth, and a foe of all that smacked of efficiency and progress. Not for me the dreary calculations of maximized yields per acre; I would go for quality production, not quantity. With a vast, idealistic counterculture just sinking its teeth into the greening of America, I aimed to be right in the vanguard of agriculture.

Local folks were puzzled. *Organic* refers to certain methods of farming, but not to any particular variety of farming. What they had wanted to know was, would I be a dairy farmer? Corn farmer? Pig farmer? In short, what sort of crops or critters did I plan to raise? I had no ready answers, but the subject seemed prosaic indeed compared to what was on my mind. Why, I could have written an impassioned essay about organic versus chemical farming from the qualified perspective of an expert. An authentic farm owner. It hardly seemed important that I had not grown a thing, yet.

Eventually, I figured out that I would be a *sheep* farmer, which meant that I was also going to be a *hay* farmer. Sheep eat hay — all winter long — and the stuff sells for roughly twice the money that it costs to produce. I acquired twenty-year-old models of the proper tools — mower, baler, rake — to go along with my twenty-year-old tractor. Then I waited for spring to make my hay crop grow.

In the farm press, my fellow tillers of the soil were complaining vehemently. Fertilizer prices were heading up — way up. How could a farmer today afford to feed his crops? Complaints aside, I noticed that my neighbors were buying fertilizer in loads that made their heavy-duty pickup trucks steer like battleships. Then, for hours on end, they would drive their tractors round and round their fields, broadcasting the stuff.

I visited one of these backward compatriots to get the tongue welded on my 1954 hay baler, and there, in the far bay of his machinery shed, stood a small mountain of bagged fertilizer. Corn starter, superphosphate, urea, muriate of potash, ammonium phosphate — there were hundreds of bags, and I had read that each bag cost between four and six dollars.

"Wow!" I said. "You really believe in fertilizer, don't you?"

He said: "Costs a lot of money. But you can't harvest what you didn't grow."

Now here, I thought, was an open invitation to enlighten a fellow farmer. To explain a better, a New Age way. I said, "I'm into *organics*. I think we all ought to try to *love* the soil — *care* for it, *nurture* it. Not get the soil addicted to these chemical stimulants. Why, they're just like pushing drugs!"

"I like to see crops grow," he said.

"Me, too! Me, too! But I think our plants will learn to grow more healthy, more disease-free — more nutritious, too — if we just create a natural environment and . . . "

"Well," he said, "it's time to do my chores. I hope you'll excuse me."

It is always hard to change the conventional wisdom. I had a worse disillusionment, however, when I went to a powwow of local organic farmers. Half a dozen of them. Carrot growers, strawberry growers — that sort of farmer. They met every spring to pool orders for fertilizer — of all things! — so that they could obtain their needs in wholesale quantities. The difference between them and my neighbors was that they used *organic* fertilizers. Wood ashes. Dried kelp. Tankage and bone meal.

Dried kelp, in Vermont, is a frightfully expensive way to fertilize a crop. It may pay its way in an intensive market garden, with the produce sold at health food stores, but you certainly can't spread it on a hay field of several acres. In short, organic farming with organic fertilizers seemed a far more expensive and complicated proposition than organic farming *without* organic fertilizers. Without any fertilizer at all, in fact: a triumph of philosophy over activity. Philosophy, I couldn't help reflecting, was dirt cheap.

While I was philosophizing, we endured a May that was remarkably deficient in rainfall. "Rain in May," the adage goes, "means a barn full of hay"; now I could see plainly that the converse was also true. Where my neighbors would normally expect to mow some eighty bales per acre — two tons — they were gloomily predicting yields of only fifty. My fields, naturally, didn't seem as thick as theirs. But I had no standard of comparison to past years, and, besides, I liked my rather short, well-spaced, honest grasses. They might be a trifle stunted, but at least there was nothing *hyper* about them.

When I mowed this crop, my aged sickle-bar performed effortlessly. When I raked it up, I had to merge half a dozen broad swaths together just to make a windrow of modest width and height. And when I ran the baler up and down those windrows, I found myself putting up six bales to the acre. Six. Three hundred pounds of hay — about *one-tenth* of an average farmer's average yield.

When a person's hay fields adjoin a public highway — as mine do — yields on the order of six bales per acre just do not go unnoticed. "You know," a neighbor couldn't help pointing out, "it costs you something to drive those machines around your field whether there's any hay there or not."

"This is *organic* hay," I protested. "Never been fertilized."

"I doubt if your sheep are going to know the difference. And anyway, you're going to have to buy a lot of hay besides this to get them through the winter. And it won't be organic, either."

He had a point — although, I learned in the next few years, one can buy organic hay or organic just-about-anything if one really wants it. All one has to do is ask the seller: "Is this organic?" and appear prepared to pay a premium for same. The answer will nearly always be yes. Cynicism aside, though, when I pushed a pencil on the cost of my organic hay crop I was fairly staggered. I had kept the inputs low, but there was no output. I had spent one hundred hours — and one hundred hours in the waning life of my machinery — doing almost nothing.

If there is one thing I'm accomplished at, it is overreacting to perceived mistakes and past failings. I went out and bought a thick textbook on soils and soil fertility — and I *read* it. I bought a soil auger and sent many cores of my plow layer to a laboratory. I pored over their advice. Basically, I had a nitrogen deficiency because the clover in my fields had run out, giving way to grasses. I could plow the fields up and reseed to new legumes, which make their own nitrogen by accommodating friendly bacteria on their roots, or I could top-dress the existing stand of grasses with nitrogen fertilizer. Or I could give up.

Taking the path of least effort, I swallowed my ideological scruples and went shopping for some bagged nitrogen fertilizer. There were several types. The cheapest kind, urea, was a good bet for top-dressing only if rains arrived shortly after application; otherwise it would be lost to the atmosphere rather than sink into the soil and do some good. Ammonium phosphate, another kind, included a lot of phosphorus that I didn't think I needed. Finally I settled on ammonium nitrate, a rather expensive but stable and quick-acting variety of nitrogen.

"How much of this you going to spread to the acre?" the fertilizer dealer asked me.

I showed him my soil test results. "What would you recommend?"

He scratched his head, studying the printout. "Fifty pounds of nitrogen per acre ought to grow a hay crop."

"Good," I said. "In that case, I think I'll spread one hundred pounds."

His eyes widened. "You're not playing around, are you?"

"Nope," I said — just another yeoman farmer. "You can't harvest what's not there. Me, I like to see crops grow."

Ammonium nitrate is thirty-four percent actual nitrogen; to put one hundred pounds of N on a given acre, I had to spread three hundred pounds of granulated fertilizer. And I had no tractor-driven spreader. I *did* have an old-fashioned broadcast seeder, a canvas bag that hung from my shoulder by a frayed strap. While I walked and turned a crank, fertilizer pellets would dribble onto a whirling plate and be scattered across a twenty-foot swath. Low, low tech.

It took me two days to fertilize seven acres this way; when I had finished, one shoulder was distinctly lower than my other. But we had appropriate growing weather throughout the last three weeks of May, and it was soon apparent that I had a monster hay crop growing. Thick. Tall. Green.

Quality hay is early-cut hay, and by month's end I had greased my mower and made an attempt to wade into the hay field with it. Nothing doing. Within moments it had plugged, and plugged again. Then its Pitman arm — a crucial link in the drive train fashioned, on that old machine, of white oak to withstand vibration — this ancient Pitman arm cracked and was reduced to splinters. End of first attempt at mowing.

In the dingy cellar of a local farm machinery dealer, a parts man unearthed three old wooden Pitman arms. I bought him out, and broke each one in short order. By the time I broke the last one, I had circumnavigated my amazing hay field twice.

I visited my neighbor and implored him to bail me out with his mammoth, ultramodern, heavy-duty mowing rig. He promised to work my field into his schedule. A week or so later, his machine pulled up my driveway. "That's some crop," he said admiringly. "And that's organic?"

"Well, almost," I said. "I used a bit of nitrogen."

He revved the mower up and entered my field at the hay-cutting speed to which he was accustomed — and almost immediately his machine was plugged. Badly. He shut down, and together we pulled green hay from the sickles.

"Thick!" he grunted. "Guess I'd best slow down."

He hit the stand again in a lower gear, but the mower plugged and we had to clean it out again. Then he put the big machine in a gear so low that it crept along, considerably slower than a man can crawl. An enormous quantity of hay spewed out behind it. Many hours later, he had finished. It was nearly dark. But he came to find me and demanded: "How *much* nitrogen?"

I told him.

"Lord God," he said. "You better have a laboratory test that hay. *Before* you feed it. There is such a thing as nitrate poisoning."

"Oh?"

"I hope your rake will rake that. And you better buy a pile of shear pins for your baler. Anyway," he said, "it's mowed."

I *did* have the hay tested, and it proved to be nontoxic. There is also, however, a Law of Diminishing Returns in fertilizer application; once my hay was in the barn, I had to admit that I had violated this law flagrantly. Immoderate stimulation of a crop with nitrogen does produce impressive yields, but it is not apt to maximize profits.

Now, many years later, I am resigned, every May, to the annual performance of fertility rites. I've learned to bring a measure of temperance to these efforts, and to utilize the magical substances with some wisdom and respect. I never plan to do without them, though. And when people ask me whether farmers can still feed the world, my answer is confident: if the inputs can be purchased at a price that justifies their use, farmers can grow so much damn food that nobody would believe it.

• Terminal Sire

A person trades his car in when it can no longer climb steep hills, and a few summers ago I made the painful admission that my seven-year-old ram was having climbing problems, too. He seemed out of gas, or out of whatever libidinous fuel had driven him to sire a cool five hundred lambs or better. The old boy was still reasonably competent to hobble across the barnyard and delight a waiting ewe; he had not given up completely. But I could no longer turn him out to cruise a sprawling pasture and expect my flock of sheep to be reliably bred.

I recalled the day when I had purchased Mister Right from a

farmer fifty miles away. He was no spring chicken, no pig in a poke; he was nearly four years old and a thoroughly proven terminal sire. Terminal sires are used to produce meat lambs for the butcher rather than breeding stock; they excel at muscling and frame size and conformation. At my barn, I wrestled the enormous animal off my truck and into a pen made out of hardwood pallets. Not twenty minutes later, he had bashed his way right through the wall of the barn, crashed a pasture gate, and trotted out to introduce himself to several bored and jaded ewes. They seemed utterly impressed.

Now the old fellow could scarcely have smashed his way out of a cardboard carton. I confined him with a couple of hurdles so flimsy that it practically made me cry, and then, sadly, I went shopping.

Buying a ram used to be essentially a matter of choosing a pretty face, or a well-turned leg, and hoping for the best. Comparisons of size and rate of development between rams from different flocks were relatively meaningless, since nutritional inputs and environmental stresses vary tremendously from one farm to another. True, any ram lamb sold for breeding purposes would have to be exceptional in the flock of origin. But there was no fair way to ask, Compared to what?

All that has changed, in recent years, with the advent of Ram Performance Tests now carried out annually at several land-grant colleges and agricultural experiment stations. Ram tests are, in a sense, the ultimate pie-eating contest; premier breeders consign promising young bucks to a central test station, where technicians feed them all they are willing to consume of a pelleted-grain diet formulated for optimum growth. The environment, compared to that of an average farm, is consistently immaculate. There is no muck or mud, no flies doing the backstroke in a trough of stagnant water, no exposure to internal parasites or worms. All the ram lambs have to do is shuffle around their clean pens and gorge themselves on something analogous to spinach ice cream.

Every couple of weeks, each ram is weighed; weight gains are then tallied against the quantity of feed consumed in order to arrive at figures on feed conversion for each animal. Rate of gain and feed conversion ability are heritable traits of profound economic importance, and a terminal sire imparts them in some measure to each of his offspring. There are rams that only manage to gain one-half pound per day on four to five pounds of feed; and there are rams that gain a pound a day on three pounds of feed, or less. The latter type of ram, when it can be objectively identified, is worth a great deal of money in a breeding program.

At the end of eight to fourteen weeks, depending on the particular ram test, the outstanding rams are typically offered at an auction sale. It was to just such a sale that I went. The late-summer day was hot and muggy, and the rams were displayed in an enormous, sweltering barn where not a breath of air moved. Beer was available — a sound aid to enhancing auction prices — and much was consumed. For several hours two hundred shepherds eyeballed twenty rams and shared deeply felt critiques concerning the finer points of style and conformation. The rams, all washed and combed and gussied up, stared back uncomprehendingly. But I stuck to the facts on the computer printout of the test and found myself coveting the top-gaining Suffolk ram.

He never would have won a show; he lacked the height and length and scale that modern Suffolk breeders strive for. But Suffolk breeding has become a class of sporting event, and its current goal appears to be to grow a five-hundred-pound sheep. Toward this cause, the ram I was attracted to would have been worthless, but he had put on a whopping 1.51 pounds of gain per day over a period of twelve weeks. And he had a set of legs that just wouldn't quit.

There are people who can bid without emotion at an auction, and I am not one of them. Not for me the imperceptible nod, the quick wink or shrug that ratchets prices upward without betraying who is interested. No, I *wanted* that ram, and I hoped that a display of my determination would discourage others. Such was not the case. One bidder dropped out at $180, and another quit at $245, but a third one battled me in five-dollar increments right up to $320. For a *sheep* — and for a ram lamb who was not show material and whose breeding ability was still wholly a matter of speculation.

Three hundred dollars had been my limit. Now, unwilling to bid $325, I folded.

"Look again!" the auctioneer shouted. "You've just owned him for the last ten minutes, and didn't it feel nice? Now, for five dollars, you can own him for a while longer!"

Somehow — too much heat, or beer? — this proposition

made good sense. I raised my bidder's card again. And now the opposition folded, probably surmising that I was not bidding rationally and therefore could not be beaten. The auctioneer whacked his hammer on the podium, and the winner of the pie-eating contest was mine.

I got him home, and penned him in the barn, and old Mister Right reacted in the manner of England's George III, when, on his deathbed, his son was ushered in wearing coronation gowns. England's king sat right up, got well, and reigned for thirty more years; the king of my barnyard snorted and tossed his head and pawed the ground like any young buck spoiling for a fight. But I would not let him have it, for his own sake. His old bones were far too brittle.

The new ram — Fat Boy, I called him — soon exhibited a remarkable appetite for grain. He regarded hay and pasture with utter disdain. He had, after all, acquired a college degree in eating; he knew what he liked. To operate on pasture, though, it is helpful for a ram to be a little bit lean and mean, and it is crucial that he be capable of handling the feed out there. Bluegrass, not barley. Clover, not corn.

We struggled to achieve a dietary compromise, and after several weeks I had him down to a mere three pounds of grain a day. And it was October: time to turn him loose to breed my ewes. I painted his chest so that he'd mark the sheep he mounted — a simple way to check up on a ram's activity — and led him out to meet the girls. The girls ran away from him, which is not uncommon. What was uncommon was that he did not follow them. Not for long, anyway. He went back to the barnyard and started bellowing for grain.

Frankly, I was disappointed. I enjoy a good meal as much as anybody, but on my scale of values gustatory pleasure just doesn't compete with passion. Since he would not chase the ewes, I was determined that I would chase the ewes to him. I rounded them up and drove them to the barnyard and shut the gate to confine them with Fat Boy. Close quarters. No escaping. Fat Boy looked up, and sniffed the air with interest.

A good ram — not a great one, but a sound breeder who knows the ropes — ought in such circumstances to service eight ewes in the first twenty minutes. After twenty minutes, my Fat Boy had not serviced anyone; but he *had* fallen in love. Callow and romantic, he stared into her eyes and pressed her, cheek-to-cheek, and flicked his tongue. She stood waiting for something else to happen, and eventually — about an hour later — it did. Over the next day and a half he mounted her repeatedly, to the absolute exclusion of all others.

"I have a monogamous ram!" I complained to an older and rather more experienced shepherd. "And after what I paid for him, whatever lambs I get are going to turn out damned expensive!"

He came to see. The rump of Fat Boy's wife was completely smeared with marking paint, while not one other ewe out of a hundred had been touched. "Well," he said, "tomorrow she'll be out of heat, and I expect he'll find another. And so forth."

"It'll take *months* to get this flock bred at that rate!"

"How old is the ram?"

"Seven months."

"Well, he's enormous for his age. But he hasn't got the world's biggest testicles."

What kind of a crack was *that*, I wondered. A crude remark, a low insult to this fine creature whose superior growth rate had been so meticulously documented. "What's the matter with his testicles?"

"You measured them?"

"What do you mean, measure them?" I sputtered. Of all the sick, weird, perverted . . .

"When a ram lamb is mature enough to breed, his testicles ought to be twelve inches in circumference."

"Twelve inches!"

"You got a tape measure handy?"

We caught the ram — all it took was waving a pail of grain — and my friend made a quick, deft measurement. He said: "I'm afraid you've sent a boy to do a man's job. Maybe next month. Maybe next year. He's just not ready yet."

"What am I supposed to do?"

"You've still got your old ram, haven't you?"

"Yes, but he can hardly get around."

"Let me check *his* testicles."

So I got a lesson in examining the business end of a ram. Mister Right may have been old and tired, but he had the supple and well-toned — and enormous — equipment of a terminal sire in his prime. "If he can't work for you on pasture," advised my friend, "keep him in the barn and just run the ewes in with him every night. I'll bet he covers every one in a couple of weeks."

So Mister Right got to sire a final crop of lambs. Each morning, the old boy looked ready for a blood transfusion; but he did not fail at his nightly work, and I kept Fat Boy penned where he could watch and maybe pick up a pointer or two. The next year Fat Boy took over the job and proved perfectly equal to it. He even kicked the grain habit, eventually. But I still keep Mister Right — a true geezer, nowadays — over in the corner waiting. Just in case the new ram fails. Somehow, I don't think the old boy's quite over the hill.

• Synchronicity

Trying to get hold of a shepherd in March can be as hard as finding a shrink in August. Not, however, because shepherds are on holiday; on the contrary, they have taken up quarters in their lambing barns to preside over the consequences of the previous October's blithe copulations. Seasonal reproductive habits in sheep, marketing patterns, and climatic factors all combine to make March an ideal month for lambing; and shepherds who make good are adamant about giving their flocks undivided attention during this crucial harvest.

When the first lambs hit the ground, a shepherd is apt to wax poetic about the miracle of birth, the wonder of maternal love, and similar romantic themes. Before very long, though, he waxes exhausted. And furious at lambs too dumb to suckle, ewes too arrogant to own what they have borne, and the general tendency for living things to run amok. Obstetric problems crop up when one least expects them; mothers will unwittingly lie down on their fragile offspring; the biggest and flashiest lamb will gambol into a water trough and drown. Then all a shepherd wants is a hot bath, a hot meal, and a full night's sleep; but if he succumbs to satisfying such desires, things will have gone from bad to worse by the time he gets back on duty.

Every shepherd has a tale of catching forty winks when no ewes appeared to be in labor, and then waking up to find dead lambs scattered in the snow. Such memories make for troubled sleep.

Tramp into a shepherd's barn at the *end* of lambing season, and one is apt to find a person fit to be committed. Wild-eyed, hair unkempt, clothes caked with dried blood and amniotic fluid, fingers raw from iodine and weird obstetric lubricants — such a person, even if hard-pressed, could scarcely spell his name. But such a person will be apt to say what shepherds say each year: dang it, there has got to be a better way to go through lambing.

Talk like that is cheap, and only lasts for a couple of weeks in most cases. Our memories of fatigue, like most pain, are blessedly short-lived. But I have a colleague in the Yankee shepherd biz who vowed, a few years ago, never to lamb out his one hundred eighty ewes on *their* time ever again. He would make them do it *his* way. Combining old ideas and new technologies in a bold, creative fit, he cooked up a scheme to have three forty-eight-hour lambing periods — sixty ewes at a shot — spaced at two-week intervals. March 1–2, March 15–16, and March 30–31: he could even circle the dates on his calendar. In between these stints of frenzied lambing, he would be at home catching up on sleep.

"How?" I asked him, overawed. "How on earth?"

"Elementary." He reviewed, briefly, the hard facts of ovine reproduction: sixteen-day average estrus or heat cycle, with fertility for roughly two days of the cycle; twenty-one-week average gestation, with about a week of variation — longer or shorter — among individual sheep. With a ratio of one ram to fifty ewes, one could expect one's flock to become substantially bred in three weeks' time.

But I knew all this, and I knew what the results were like each March. "What can you do differently?" I asked my wise friend. "Change their heat cycles?"

"People *are* doing that, in France," he said. "With hormone-soaked pessaries. I've got something simpler, though: if you know, within a day or two, when a ewe got bred, then you can induce her to lamb twenty weeks later. Without serious prematurity."

"So what are you going to do, run around for three weeks in October with a clipboard, recording who gets bred on what day?"

"No. I'm going to smear some wedding paint on the rams' chests."

"*Wedding* paint?"

"That's what the English call it. You know — just a smear of paint and old crankcase oil. So that every time a ram mounts a ewe, he marks her back."

"Swell," I said. "But still, you won't know . . . "

"Wait. Just listen. I paint the rams, and I put them in with the ewes for five days. Then I pull them out. Now, every ewe who's got a paint mark — and that ought to be about one-third of them — can be induced in one hundred and forty days. Assuming she looks pregnant."

"Induce them *how?*"

"With dexamethasone. It's a steroid, and it — somehow it mimics whatever the fetus puts out to get labor going. You give them a shot, and they lamb within twenty-four to seventy-two hours. They just *do.*"

Now I caught the genius of it. "And for forty-eight hours, you can stay on top of things, right? You can put each ewe in a pen by herself, and you'll *know* there won't be any lambs out in the snow, and . . . "

"I think you could even just about pick your *weather,*" he said. "Within a day or two of the target dates. Like you wouldn't have to be out lambing in a blizzard."

"You *sure* you want to see one hundred lambs hit the ground in a couple of days?"

"Sure I'm sure," he said. "Because I'm going to have people like you there to help me do it."

"Paying combat wages?"

"No, but I will get a keg of beer. Chips and pretzels. Pizza. I will move the stereo out into the barn — with the *good* speakers, too — and we will have a lambing party."

"Go on!"

"What, you wouldn't come? Don't you want to see if synchronicity works?"

"What about the *other* hundred and twenty ewes?"

He tapped his forehead proudly; he had thought of everything. "Sixteen days after the rams come out, I put them back in. For five more days. With a different color paint. That group of ewes gets induced a couple of weeks later. And then, sixteen days from the second time the rams came out — well, you get the picture?"

"Eureka!" I said. "Count me in."

Of course, I could only be counted in for the first of his three lambing bashes, because after that I had my own barn to attend to. But I looked forward to a glimpse of his brave new world, eager to see whether he was onto something brilliant or whether one more elegant conception would degenerate into problematic realities.

First of March, he called to say he didn't like the weather forecast. Same thing on the second. This, I thought, was just like *haying*; injecting dexamethasone into sixty pregnant ewes was analogous to mowing a hay field down, and he was waiting for a forecast of three fair days. On the third of March, though, a couple of his ewes lambed spontaneously. He could wait no longer, and the weather forecast was actually promising. So I threw a change of overalls into my pickup truck and headed over the mountains to his farm.

Just as haying forecasts often go awry, this one did, too, and I arrived in the midst of sporadic snow flurries and blustery winds. By nightfall it was ten degrees and snowing to beat hell. But the ewes had been induced, and now there was no turning back.

Two other shepherds soon arrived. The four of us were experienced ovine obstetricians, to be sure; but we also proved experienced and dedicated beer drinkers. By midnight, with a dozen ewes settling down to earnest labor, three of us were staggering around trying to find a way to keep the keg from freezing. And the fourth lamber was curled up in his sleeping bag.

"Lishen," said the host. "We could pack the keg in fresh manure and bedding. Stuff must throw some heat."

"It's the *tap* that's freezhing," my compatriot countered.

"Get some of those heat lamps that we use to dry off lambs," I said. There *were* half a dozen heat lamps, but now I set in motion an enduring conflict between whether to use the things to warm lambs or thaw beer. At times, over the next two days, it became a tough decision.

Finally, lambs began to hit the ground — all at once. In conventional lambing schemes, two or more ewes often seem to pace each other's labors and deliver simultaneously; but in my friend's system of synchronicity, when it rained it poured. At one point, thirty-seven lambs were born within a couple of hours. Each had to be squared away — weighed, recorded, have its umbilical cord clipped and disinfected, shown where the milk was waiting, and helped to fill its stomach — and more than a few had to be revived at birth from mechanical pneumonia caused by fluid in the lungs.

This is agreeable work — and work that can be performed in a state of mild inebriation — at the rate of about three lambs per hour. At twenty lambs per hour, in the hands of raving, freezing drunkards, singing golden oldies in four-part harmony along with an outsize stereo's booming speakers, the average newborn must have wondered what the hell kind of world he had wandered into.

But it *was* a better deal than being born out in the snow, or in an unattended barn. By the second night, the storm had broken and we were well along toward finishing our work. There was time to sleep, in shifts, and help ourselves to a sumptuous buffet in the shepherd's house. I even got a shower. But toward midnight, another run of lambs was plainly on the way, and we all four roused ourselves to meet it.

I climbed in a pen to help a ewe that had been laboring fruitlessly for several hours already. Making an inspection, I reached into her uterus and dragged out the skull of a well-decayed fetus. Mummified, in fact. This is not the rarest of occurrences, but it is always an unsettling one; it indicates that a reasonably well-formed lamb somehow died within the womb, long enough ago that nonbony structures have decomposed into a goopy, white gel. Incredibly, in sheep this can happen without jeopardizing sibling fetuses, though they may be born quite weak.

So I threw aside the skull and reached back in to find another lamb. *Most* of a lamb, that is. I felt hoofs, legs, torso, tail, hindquarters — I felt everything possible except a head. "Oh, no," I said. "Oh, no."

"You need a beer?"

"I think I have a headless lamb."

"Headlesh? Thass impossible!"

"*You* check."

Over the next half hour, each of us entered that ewe and reconnoitered things. Nobody could find a head. "I thought I had a rotten one, see?" I said, showing the skull. "But maybe there was an accident, maybe the head just came off — just separated — and the body healed at the neck and the fetus kept on growing . . . "

"Headlesh or not, we've got to get that lamb out of there."

"You try," I suggested.

Eventually we *all* tried. And our unsuccessful efforts yielded a new theory: when a lamb has lost its head *in utero*, the shoulders become unnaturally well developed and hence undeliverable.

"Fetotomy," the host declared.

"Whass that?"

"Taking it out in pieces. Only way. Let me get a sharp knife."

"Holy. . . wait a minute," I protested. "It's been a swell party, but . . . shouldn't we call a vet?"

Calling a vet, to shepherds who pride themselves on obstetric competency, is a damning admission of defeat. But I prevailed on my friends because, frankly, I thought we had collectively overdosed on lambing. And I had this quiet misgiving powerfully confirmed when, at four in the morning, a local veterinarian stumbled into the barn with kit in hand. There we were — beery, bleary, smelling like old placentas and surrounded by ninety-odd lambs whose births we had so recently celebrated. "Where's this headless lamb?" he asked, taking in the scene with genuine surprise.

"Over there. In *her*."

He washed up and climbed into the ewe's pen and reached inside her, as we all began to explain about the disembodied skull, the Accident Theory, the Big Shoulder Theory, and much else. When we finished, he said: "Can't say I've ever heard of headless lambs before. Now. . . " He twisted something deep inside the ewe — in up to his armpit — and worked something sideways, and reached around a different way, and suddenly he smiled and dragged out a baby lamb. *With* a head. Alive. Distressed — no doubt about it — but very much alive.

"Gee whiz!"

"Wow!"

"Amazing!"

"There's your headless lamb," he said. The lamb drooled and shook its head as its long-suffering mother turned around to lick it. "You'd have been mighty sorry to do a fetotomy."

I said, "Well, I thought I'd seen it all. Where was that head hiding?"

"Tucked down on the chest. And twisted. Don't see that too often," he said. "Well, that's fifteen dollars. You boys party this way right through lambing?"

"We only lamb for two days at a time," the host said.

"Two days, huh? All these lambs were born in two days?"

"We do it with drugs. And synchronicity. I got sick of having to lamb all month long, every March."

"Two days?" He shook his head. "Looks like that's been just about a day and a half too long." And with that he wished us a good morning and left the barn.

We never even finished the manure-packed keg — though I daresay *someone* finished it — and after a morning nap I set off for home and my own imminent lambing season. Month-long. Low-tech. Totally unsynchronized and, as usual, exhausting. But I had seen the future, and the future had had, well, some real problems of its own.

• Castration Anxiety

Few newborn creatures seem as perfectly proportioned, as delicately wrought, and as gladdening to the heart and eye as a baby lamb. Even after a solid decade of shepherding — even after caring for well over a thousand of them — I still manage to spend hours of infinite enjoyment watching new lambs undertake to learn the ropes of life. Typically, they first manage to wobble to their feet within ten minutes of birth, an accomplishment so startling that it makes perfectly normal human babies seem like morons in comparison. Then, with or without their mother's aid, they find her hidden faucets and discover how to make them work. By three days of age they can prance and gambol, jump and climb; they have all the skills they need to reconnoiter the great world.

Unfortunately, newborn lambs are *not* perfectly formed — not, at any rate, from the point of view of meat production. Every single one of them has an unwanted tail, and generally half of them have two unwanted testicles. Troublesome appendages. So, within the first days or weeks of a lamb's life, one of a shepherd's less poetic tasks is to amputate the undesired parts of each of them. Cutting off the tail is called *docking* an animal, and cutting off the testicles is called — guess what? Castration.

On first learning of these bizarre responsibilities, I was more than a little incredulous. I had chanced upon a U.S. Department of Agriculture publication, Leaflet 551: *Docking, Castrating, and Ear Tagging Lambs;* I remember feeling a brief moment of surprise that my government had found time to be interested in these matters. (Nowadays, nothing surprises me.) According to this booklet, the chief reasons for making a lamb's tail disappear were:

1. Docked lambs are much cleaner around the tail and are much less susceptible to fly strike and maggot infestation.
2. Docking improves the general appearance of lambs and sheep.
3. Docked or short-tailed ewes are easier to breed and settle.
4. The dressed carcasses of docked lambs are more attractive in appearance.
5. Packers and lamb feeders pay higher prices for docked lambs.

Since, by temperament and by education, I attempt to bring a critical faculty to bear upon authoritative pronouncements of any sort, I sat down and analyzed this list of reasons carefully. Reasons two and four were in fact identical — a "reason" based entirely upon an aesthetic judgment that, for all I knew, might change tomorrow as surely as hemlines or hairstyles or any other element of fashion. Reason number three seemed patently absurd — if the tails of animals actually interfered with reliable breeding, few mammalian species would have made it this far down the evolutionary turnpike. I felt sure that any willing ewe and desiring ram, caught in the heat of passion, would find a way to get around whatever inconvenience a mere tail might pose.

As to reason number one, I considered maggot infestation frankly a remote concern, given reasonable practices of cleanliness in husbandry. Again, I raised the evolutionary argument: if these tails were such an all-fired liability, how had the species managed to retain them for lo, all these millennia?

Reason number five, however, was a real stinker. I failed to dock my first year's lambs and, sure enough, *I* was docked two dollars per head when it came time to market them. "Why?" I demanded of the packer, hunched over his scale.

"Because people don't *eat* tails, that's why. I should pay you sixty-two cents a pound, liveweight, for something I'm just going to chuck?"

"It couldn't weigh more than a pound and a half," I argued.

"Yes, but do you know what's on it? Fat."

"So what?"

"You leave the tail on a lamb, and as it grows the animal lays down fat on it. But if there's *no* tail, that same fat would get laid down someplace I could use it. On the loin or leg, see? Someplace I could sell it to the next guy for a lot of money. You don't dock the tail, you make the entire carcass less valuable to me."

While he was at it, he counted up the number of ram lambs on my load and docked me *three* dollars per head on them. Testicles.

"Come on," I said. "I *know* there are people who eat those. Call them Rocky Mountain oysters or something, right?"

"Now and again I do sell them," he admitted. "But that isn't the point. Ram lambs with testicles are harder for my men to skin. The hide don't pull off so easy. I don't know why, but it slows the whole kill line down — and that costs me *at least* three dollars. Those guys on the kill line make good pay."

Not like me, I thought. And here, I couldn't help noting, was hard evidence that there are fundamental differences between males and females. Not much to cling to in an age of sexual equality — of unisex — but there it was: the males are not so easily skinned.

But any way I looked at it, the packer's economic argument seemed incontrovertible. When a person has produced a hundred-pound lamb worth sixty-two dollars at a cost of, let's say, *fifty* dollars, he cannot afford to have five bucks taken out for the presence of a tail and testicles. So, before my next crop of baby lambs hit the ground, I consulted a catalogue of livestock supplies and discovered an astonishing array of tools designed to make the testicles and tails of farm livestock disappear.

There was, for example, the Double Crush White's Emasculator — a foot-long, fearsome-looking cross between surgical scissors and a lineman's beefy pliers. Then there was the Electric Docker, 110-volt vise grips that would cauterize the flesh on the stump of tail left behind, minimizing any risk of infection. Then there was the All-In-One Instrument, a cunning little gadget that could snip off a scrotal sac, haul out testicles, zip off tails, and even cut notches in a lamb's ears, should one want to do that.

Fascinated and repulsed, I let my attention turn to a rather less dramatic, less immediately decisive tool. Elastrator, it was cleverly called. What it did was spread a tiny rubber band wide open, so it could be slipped over an unsuspecting tail or scrotum. Once released from the tool, the band would cut off circulation to the affected part; said appendage would, over a period of days or weeks, atrophy and slough off with no bloody moment of excision. Like a foot going to sleep — but for good. The tool was alleged to be particularly humane and painless, but the same claim was made for all the other castrators, too.

It sounded right for me. I ordered an Elastrator and a few hundred of the special little rubber bands. Come the day for docking and castration, and I found that I could breeze through the first job but the second required four hands: one to hold the squirming lamb, one to hold the Elastrator, and two to try to coax the baby testicles into their sac and hold them there until the rubber band was released. I appealed to my wife to help me with this gruesome work, and together we deepened our relationship over the course of a completely frustrating afternoon. In a state of nervousness and — dare I say it? — apprehension, nearly every male lamb would hoist its testicles far up into its abdomen. *Far* up. The more they were teased and pinched and manipulated, the greater became their desire to stay there. But when we could work them down, immediately I felt like a deceitful brute. A sexual con artist. *Sproing!*

One thing about the little rubber castrating bands: once you have released one from the Elastrator, you don't get it off again. No second chances, whether you have done the desired job or not. My wife and I produced a perfectly weird assortment of lambs with no testicles — true wethers — lambs with just one testicle in half a sac, lambs with two stunted testicles lolling in their paunch, and several other distressing variations on this theme of general incompetence.

There has to be a better way, I said. And then I heard about another amazing tool, the Burdizzo Emasculator. From Italy, where they make things right. It cost about a hundred dollars, weighed about five pounds, and looked like a . . . well, like a blacksmith's tongs in stainless steel with specialized, flattened five-inch jaws. Clamped over a scrotum, what it did was crush the spermatic cord to each testicle without otherwise insulting the lamb. No blood. No amputation. Once the cords had been properly crushed, the testicles would simply not develop.

I paid the hundred dollars and received the Burdizzo Emasculator in the mail. This tool must certainly belong in a museum of arcane devices thought up and produced by the human race. But using it — for an amateur, anyway — turned out to be a *three-person job: one to hold the lamb, one to work a testicle down into the sac, and one to administer the enormous crushing force of this tool with its twelve-inch handles. For the extra hands, my wife and I enlisted her mother, one fine winter's morn. After half an hour, we could have used a fourth person — a professional therapist, say — to counsel us and give us psychological support as we emasculated our way through fifty-odd lambs. I can't think of any less agreeable way to spend a morning on the farm.

The next year, come castration time, I happened to have a visiting shepherd from Montana on the farm for a few days. Checking out the Yankee sheep scene. He couldn't believe that I had spent one hundred dollars on a Burdizzo Emasculator; he took me to the barn and showed me how it's done out West. I would hold a lamb. He would slice off the lower scrotum with his penknife in a flash, then pull the little testicles out with his teeth and spit them into a nearby pail. Not only was this quick and efficient, my observation was that it was far less painful and disturbing to the lambs than the tortures I had put them through.

The next year, it would have been my turn to do the knife-and-teeth bit; I can just imagine inviting my wife's help with *that*. But a funny thing happened — or, rather, I learned that a funny thing had been happening all along. Carefully evaluating several years of feeding records, I discovered my *castrati* didn't grow as fast as the lambs that, in my first year, I had left intact. Not only did they fail to grow as fast, they failed to grow as *well*. They put on less lean and more fat. They were not ideally muscled. And they made me swallow increased feed costs for a decreased rate of daily gain.

I asked a local livestock expert about these matters. "Sure," he said, "everybody knows that happens with castration."

"Well, what can I do about it?"

"Do?"

"These guys are *costing* me."

"There's been some work done with hormones," he said. "But just think about it: first you take the testicles out of the lamb, and then you give it hormones to do what the testicles were there to do in the first place. Doesn't make much sense, huh?"

"It sounds perfectly idiotic."

"How much do you calculate you're losing in feed for gain on those wether lambs?"

I ran some numbers through my head, and guesstimated: "Four to five dollars per head."

"How much does the packer want to dock you on intact rams?"

"Three dollars per head."

He smiled. "Think you'd be two bucks better off to not castrate, then."

Case closed. I no longer have to face castration anxiety every year, right amid all the joy and effort of lambing season. Sometimes doing nothing is the best thing one can do — and in this case, *everybody* wins.

For a while, I thought I should advertise my expensive and no longer needed castrating devices in some farm paper; maybe some other shepherd would help me recoup a portion of my investment. But then I thought: while not handy, these are certainly unusual gadgets to have around. Conversation pieces. And I thought: I have a lovely daughter. In a decade or so, she'll be going out on dates. Pimpled boys will shake my hand and make embarrassed conversation as she stalls, applying makeup, and I'll say what fathers always say — what fathers said to me when *I* was the pimpled boy. "Son, I know you'll take good care of my daughter." "Oh, yes," says the boy. "Of course."

But then, for my hundred dollars, I'll be able to open a drawer of shepherding supplies and make a strong impression on him. "Son," I will say, "we men are hard to skin. Get my meaning?"

• A Slotted Floor

I first saw a slotted floor used to support livestock several years ago, on a well-equipped pig farm that has since succumbed to the dismal economics of hog production in Vermont. The floor was built of long, narrow concrete slats, each one a little wider on the top than on the bottom; when a porker made a mess — as porkers are wont to do — the offensive effluents would find their way beneath the floor to be held in a storage area several feet deep. The animals stayed high and, if not exactly dry, at least relatively clean. And no bedding was required.

This, I thought, is Cadillac.

I began perusing educational bulletins of slotted-floor housing — bulletins from the great agricultural-science schools of the Midwest. Sheep and lambs, it turned out, were considered ideally suited for confinement on a slotted floor. By creating spatial separation between sheep and their manure, the life cycles of a number of obnoxious internal parasites — stomach worms — could be absolutely interrupted. Because the environment of a slotted floor was cooler and cleaner than that of a conventional barn floor bedded with loose hay or straw, very high animal housing densities could be achieved. And since lambs being fed for market on a slotted floor had only two significant choices as to how to spend their time — sleeping or eating — very high feed efficiencies and rates of daily gain could be expected.

I went to see my lambs on pasture, contemplating their existence. It was autumn; the best grazing had come and gone. They were burning precious calories roaming several acres of tired pasture to fill their stomachs. I thought, why not build a modest slotted floor in a portion of the barn, bring in a load of grain, and feed them out in style?

The midwestern ag schools proposed what I took to be excessively complicated slotted floor designs. Their preferred deck material was something called three-quarter-inch Number 9 unflattened expanded metal X-plate, which turned out to be not cheap. Quite commonly, their decks were perched so high above the ground that a front-end loader could clean manure from beneath while leaving the floor in place. Ingenious ventilation systems complemented these designs, so that the aroma of composting pure manure would not become the dominant environmental feature of life on the floor. All in all, the floors I studied were highly engineered affairs.

What I chose to build, though, was completely simple. I bought a pile of rough oak boards and ripped them into beveled slats on my little table saw, which protested vehemently. Terminally, in fact. Then I nailed the slats to four-by-eight-foot joist frames, so that I could assemble and disassemble the floor in sheet-of-plywood-size modules. Between each slat, I left a five-eighths-inch-wide slot — a dimension I chose after careful meditation on the average size of lambs' hoofs and the average size of their dark, dry dung pellets. I poised each completed frame atop a column of concrete blocks, creating a thirty-inch manure storage area underneath the floor. And then I ran the lambs in.

The great ag-science schools of the Midwest had determined housing densities of four square feet per lamb to be perfectly

adequate on a slotted feeding floor. At four square feet per lamb —
one hundred twenty animals in a space the size of a large living
room — my brand new floor looked like a Japanese commuter
train at rush hour. Lambs would have had to stand to eat or lie to
sleep in shifts; it was all too easy for them to relieve themselves
directly on top of each other. I reread the published bulletins: four
square feet per lamb *with no depression of performance.* This turned
out to mean that, while the lambs might not exactly like their
housing densities, they could be expected to stay healthy and
make appropriate weight gains. Humanist shepherd that I am, I
threw half the lambs out of the barn and back onto their pasture.
Then I filled the grain troughs for the hungry enjoyment of the
lambs that were left.

For the first couple days, the floor was a triumph. So much so
that I invited a neighbor farmer to come see its self-cleaning
properties. "Animals on top, and manure down below," I told this
dairyman with considerable pride. "Couple years of storage
space."

"Yessir," he said. "Reminds me of the hired man I had once.
Put him in the hired man's house with his wife and baby. When he
left, I found for two years they'd been throwing dirty Pampers
down into the cellar. No slotted floor, but I guess they had the
same idea."

"Jeezum," I said. "What'd you have to do?"

"Clean it out. Just like you will have to do here, one day. Worst
damn stink I ever met with in my life."

On my slotted floor's third day, I noticed something interesting had begun to happen. The high-grain diet, formulated to
maximize each lamb's rate of daily gain, was changing the consistency of their manure. There were fewer dry, marble-sized pellets
and considerably more slurried glop with the approximate consistency of Elmer's Glue-All. Much of this would dribble through the
slots in the floor, but a certain amount would not; this residue
caked the slats and raised the effective floor height by a percepti-
ble amount in a day's time.

I knew how to moderate the consistency of this manure:
feeding hay would set things right, although it would also compromise feed efficiency. I broke open a bale of hay, and quickly my
lambs scattered it in every direction. Here and there it plugged the
slots completely, but more often it was simply used like straw in

the adobe slab that the lambs were slowly pouring on top of my carpentry.

Still, substantial quantities of animal waste managed to work through the floor and down into the storage pit. Things had not failed totally. Then the flies began appearing — lots and lots of flies. I hung industrial-size sheets of flypaper from the rafters and found they could fill up to capacity overnight without making much of a dent in the population. Why? Intrepid shepherd that I am, I held my nose and took a crawl beneath the slotted floor. The growing pile of fresh manure was fairly alive with maggots, and mature flies could exercise their urges to fecundity in a nearly perfect environment, completely undisturbed.

A friend of a friend is a research technician at one of the great agricultural-science schools of the Midwest, and at this point I made contact with him by a long-distance phone call. "How," I demanded, "do you folks out there control flies underneath a slotted floor?"

He considered this a good question. "What's worked best for me," he said, "is raising chickens."

"Raising *chickens?*"

"Underneath the floor. They do get a little dirty, but they eat a lot of maggots, too. And the bottom line is you get one more crop to sell."

"*Chickens?* Raised on maggots in manure?"

"Usually a little grain falls down beneath the floor as well."

I thanked the fellow for his time, but declined to utilize his expertise. Cool weather, I expected, would depress insect activity sooner or later; and in fact a couple of hard frosts early in October managed to bring the fly problem under control. I have not, however, looked at fried chicken in quite the same way ever since my conversation with this bona fide ag scientist.

A couple more weeks passed. Each day the depth of manure that failed to fall beneath the floor became a little deeper; each day the floor performed a little less efficiently. But, by golly, lambs were growing at impressive rates. The best were putting on over a pound of gain per day. And then, on a night when I postponed feeding chores till well after dark, I happened to discover what *else* I had been growing. Rats.

Now, every barn has a residual, hard-core rodent population. Complete eradication of such pests is sheer fantasy. But when one actually sees them in the open, feeding at the trough alongside one's livestock, things have gone too far. True, this was at night; a haphazard bust. But, sensitized to the presence of a more-than-residual rat population, I soon began to sight them clearly in the daytime, too.

Here was a conundrum. My lambs were on a high-grain diet; grain was present *constantly*, so that they could fatten themselves to their hearts' content. Pure grain constitutes an impressive ration for rats as well. How was I to feed the one without feeding the other?

Behind the slotted floor, on the other side of an insubstantial wall, stood the pile of fifty tons of baled hay that I had made for winter. Since I had a surplus, toward the end of October I advertised to sell a few tons. My first customer threw a few bales into his pickup truck, then stopped and stared. And hollered: "Great God almighty!"

"Something wrong?" I asked politely.

"You got rats — *bad!* Just look at these here tunnels!"

Where he had exposed the interior of my haystack, I beheld an infinitely complex, multilaned, three-dimensional freeway. It extended, I eventually learned, throughout this fifty-foot-long, twenty-foot-wide, thirteen-foot-high pile of hay. All points were connected.

"I do seem to have a problem," I admitted.

"That's enough hay for me! You never heard of rat poison?"

"I don't think they'd eat it. They can eat *un*poisoned grain up on the floor, twenty-four hours a day."

"Got some good new poisons on the market. Kill rats in one bite, nearly. You need something, that's for sure."

I did go to a farm store and bought a whopping plastic bucket of a poison called, appropriately, Just One Bite. The bucket contained dozens of little waxed paper packets, each filled with the bait. I scattered four or five of these around the perimeter of the slotted floor — away from where the lambs could get it — and came back next morning. Not only was the offered bait all gone; rats had eaten through the lid of the plastic bucket and made off with every last packet of Just One Bite.

Cats began arriving out of nowhere, staking out the barn. They came thin and grew fat, but the rats were still out of control. Finally I sought a neighbor's wisdom, the same man of knowledge who had cleaned a basement full of soiled paper diapers. "I have a much-worse-than-average rat problem," I said. "*Much* worse. You know any cure?"

He pulled at one ear, he scratched his chin. "Well, you tried kerosene?"

"Kerosene? For rats?"

"It's an old farm remedy. First, you got to catch one rat. Alive. Then you got to soak him with kerosene."

"So what does *that* do?"

"Nothing, yet. But then you set him on fire and let him go."

"Huh?"

"That's right. He runs back to where he came from — to find his buddies — and in half an hour the barn burns down. And then you'll have no more rats."

This dry wit was more than I could handle. I begged: "Seriously, I'm in real trouble."

"Get those lambs to market. Shut down the soup line. Then you'll get on top."

He was right, of course. And when the lambs were gone, I spent three full days chipping away what they had slathered my boardwalk with. Then I tore the slotted floor up and claimed the pungent cache beneath it for the vegetable garden. And then I forswore another high-tech miracle of agricultural engineering. I have seen — and how! — the slotted-floor future. Nowadays, whenever I see one of my animals relieve itself out on the pasture, I have to repress an urge to walk over and shake its hand.

• Back on Grass

In New England agriculture, an idea whose time has come is apt to be an idea whose time first came and went many, many years ago. What goes around comes around. It's not just that Yankee farmers have short memories, or that they despise monotony in farming methods; advances in technology and changes in production costs keep the merry-go-round revolving. Properly restated, old ideas can sound mighty new.

Pasture, and the intensive management of pasture, are getting plenty of attention in the current farming climate. The coming thing. The new idea. I suppose it was inevitable: for several decades now, progressive farmers have been abandoning pastureland in favor of far more sophisticated systems for getting feed into livestock and getting out their wastes.

Cattle and sheep are thoroughly well-designed grazing tools, with many centuries of road testing built into them. They will happily shuffle over all types of terrain in every sort of weather, trying to assemble the perfect salad from the good earth's variegated offerings. By relieving themselves anyplace that feels good, these animals recycle nutrients to the fields that sustain them in the most simple and straightforward manner. With a little attention to the stocking rate — the population density of animals per acre — the grazing animals will, over time, shift the mixture of plants in a pasture to favor those most appropriate for the long-term sustenance of the grazing species *and* the sod. A stable, climax ecosystem.

In the face of these observations, it seems incredible that a generation's efforts at agricultural engineering have been predicated on the confinement of grazing animals in vast barns or sprawling feedlots. On New England's modern dairy farms, for example, a milking cow is never turned out to choose what she would like to eat from a pasture's complex menu. Instead, mechanically harvested feeds with a known nutritive analysis arrive in front of her nose at the end of an extremely complicated — and expensive — materials-handling system. A separate system, equally ingenious and amazing, stands ready to convey her manure out of the barn and back onto the fields from whence her lunch has come.

Tremendous human labor and capital investment are routinely applied, nowadays, to do for the dairy cow what she would perhaps prefer to do for herself. But the numbers — until recently — have made perfect sense. In confinement, the dairy cow can become a vastly more efficient unit of production. A pastured cow's lactation curve is not apt to peak above forty pints of milk per day; in a state-of-the-art barn, she may hit one hundred pints.

To understand why pastured livestock seldom set production records, imagine a suburbanite who fences in his backyard, throws out the lawn mower, and brings in a couple of sheep. The concept sounds great: grow some meat and wool, fertilize the lawn, and never have to mow again. Unbeatable. The problem is, the lawn has a wildly erratic growth curve — responding to temperature and moisture conditions, and much else besides — but the grazing pressure exerted by two sheep is relatively fixed.

Two sheep will want to eat, between them, ten pounds of grass per day. That's dry-matter grass, discounting its moisture content, which varies tremendously. On the first of June, though, a backyard in New England may actually be growing *twenty* pounds of grass per day, dry-matter basis. Since the sheep cannot keep up, a lot of grasses in the lawn get past their immature stage and try to reproduce themselves. They flower. They grow long, thick stems. They set seed. At each stage in this maturation process, they lose protein and digestibility for a grazing animal.

By the end of June, the lawn looks terrible. There are closely grazed splotches, and there are thirty-inch-tall plants. Probably there are weeds, too. But midsummer drought may all but *stop* the lawn from growing, and now the sheep will have to eat this coarse, mature, desiccated junk that is scarcely worth the digestive effort. By August, perhaps even this feed will have disappeared; the sheep will gradually lose weight until September weather gets the lawn once again growing more grass than they can handle.

This is a terrible way to run a backyard, much less a farm. But it is, in miniature, the simplest and most common pasture system — and the reason why the pasturing of livestock fell into such disfavor. The system is called *set stocking:* the size of the pasture to be grazed is fixed, and the number of animals to do the grazing is fixed, and about all one can do is hope for good luck with the weather. By hazard, set stocking occasionally offers a high plane of nutrition. More often, it simply keeps body and soul together for the grazing animal. Sometimes it will fail even to do that.

As soon as one sets out to improve on set stocking, one becomes involved in pasture management. The goal of pasture management is to keep the pasture — or the backyard — looking roughly like a lawn. Not only will this maximize nutritional qualities in the forage produced; it also maximizes growth. Like a beard, grass tends to grow in response to being clipped. The trick, then, is to keep the grazing pressure closely matched to the changing curve of forage growth. This takes nothing short of art.

An obvious way to match grazing pressure to pasture growth is to vary the number of animals as required. What the suburban backyard needs is *four* sheep in the month of June, one and one-half sheep in July, none in August, and three in September. But this is easier said than done, as much on a hundred-acre farm as in suburbia. The flock large enough to keep pace with forage in June would run up quite a feed bill when the forage stopped growing. And, if animals must be confined routinely to match grazing pressure with pasture growth, why not embrace confinement wholeheartedly and create an efficient system? Harvest the fields mechanically when the crop is at its peak, and serve up a consistent daily ration in the barn.

A less obvious way to match grazing pressure to pasture growth is to keep changing the size of the pasture. Suppose the suburban backyard were divided into fifteen or twenty little paddocks. Each paddock would contain, nominally, a day's grazing for two sheep in June. Each morning, the two sheep would be placed in a new paddock; by nightfall, there would scarcely be a blade of grass left and the ground would be covered with manure and soaked in urine. Next day, there would be a new paddock. By the end of the two- or three-week cycle, the first paddock would be regrown and ripe for grazing.

On the scale of a farm, this sensible system has two serious drawbacks. First, it requires an incredible expense in permanent fencing. Second, each pasture subdivision ought to be supplied with certain amenities. Like water. Like shade. The system can supply feed of rather high quality over a dramatically extended grazing season; but until recently few Yankee farmers thought it passed their seat-of-the-pants cost-benefit analysis.

What has changed the picture are new *fencing* technologies, chief among which is the portable electric fence. Developed in Great Britain, these fences are a mesh or net of plastic twine with stainless steel wires woven in. Polythene wands — for posts — are integral. A fifty-yard roll of the stuff weighs only ten pounds; four such rolls will fence in half an acre, which should provide a day's feed in June for sixty-odd sheep. By day's end, there would scarcely be a blade of grass left and the ground would be covered in manure and soaked in urine. Poised for regrowth. First thing in the morning, the shepherd spends twenty minutes *moving the fence* to enclose the next day's grazing.

The portable electric fence — powered by a portable electric fence charger, which is often photovoltaic — gives a shepherd utter flexibility to create pastures that are sized appropriately to the forage growth curve and the grazing pressure exerted by the flock. He can change the shape of a pasture at will; he can create long pseudopods or alleys to lend access to a watering trough or tree break, while still opening up prime grazing land just as it is needed. With a few hundred dollars' investment in these nifty nets, a person can leapfrog his animals across what had been an unmanageably large field in itty-bitty, half-acre bites — all summer long. This is, like, a miracle.

The miracle creates a bizarre daily chore, for those who subscribe to it. *I* subscribe to it. My sheep see me heading toward them from a quarter mile away and holler like starving prisoners. They know every step in my changing-of-the-fence procedure: rolling out the new rolls of netting, pushing in the slender posts, making the electrical connections at the fence charger. They even know the instant when I have to turn the charger off so that I can open the old pasture to the new without getting shocked myself. I pull back just a corner of the fence, and they pour through the breach. Then, for one more day, they dine beyond their wildest dreams.

When people ask me what I have to *do* as a shepherd, I now can tell them that I have to move a fence around each day. Naturally, they don't believe me; I can hardly believe it myself. It may take only twenty minutes, but it is a chore equal in importance to milking cows or slopping hogs, an honest-to-goodness chore that confers on me dignity and pride. True, a ten-year-old child could do it. But *I* do it, and it fills me with a sense of accomplishment even on days when very little else manages to get accomplished. One need not be a moron to delight in moronic work.

And every few months I have a fence-mending afternoon, tying knots and restretching my nets in the bright sun and feeling, for all the world, like some Mediterranean fisherman on a busy quay. People see me from the road, and I'm sure they think: "Look! He's working!" And if the work looks somewhat complicated, all the better. If I learned tomorrow that *rotational grazing* — the name of this game — had been proven to be a waste of time, I'm not sure just what I'd do to compensate for loss of status.

On the contrary, though, everything about tight, rotational grazing appears to be beneficial, and the evidence is pouring in, now, from far and wide. Forage production per acre is apt to double, doubling the carrying capacity of a farmer's pastures at a stroke. Protein in that forage is roughly doubled, meaning the lambs can be weaned at formerly unheard-of weights. Parasitism is substantially suppressed, by breaking up the cycles in which stomach worms contaminate feces and get reingested. And best of all, these tight pasture rotations encourage higher-quality plant species to take over stunted, worn-out fields. The sod is improved, and nourished.

So, in the years to come, we should see more and more New England livestock being turned out of their expensive barns and given the opportunity to graze once again. It will be an attractive sight — and the system works as well for cows as for sheep, at least in theory. Given the choice of moving fences around more or less constantly, or having to exert the same vigilance over a host of silage unloaders, augers, mixer-grinders, and endless conveyor belts, who knows how many farmers may opt for moving fences?

In this, at least, New England's shepherds, few of whom prepared themselves for such a lowly calling, are on the cutting edge of what is happening in agriculture. They are back on grass, and they are utilizing grass with a brilliant efficiency. There is something wise and right about technology creating simple alternatives to its worst excesses; in twenty years, today's high-tech confinement barns may look strange indeed. There is something wise and right, too, about watching grazing creatures *graze* — even if they are confined to postage-stamp-size pastures bounded all around by plastic twine. When they burp contentedly and shuffle to the next clump of endless salad, they can look for all the world like they were supposed to be there.

CHAPTER THREE

Machinations

NOT LONG AGO, I SPENT A WEEK-end on a Quaker retreat — on a mountaintop, just at the height of Vermont's stunning foliage season. I recollect a long conversation in which several Friends were complimenting each other on their keen abilities to apprehend nature's beauty. So many of the modern world's troubles, one of them suggested, stem from people's shortcomings in this regard. How could the appreciative faculty be better nurtured in the general populace? How could people be enabled, for example, to open their eyes and commune with trees and squirrels, rocks and clouds?

Our problem today, said another, pressing the point further, is that we have lost our sense of partnership with nature. Modern man is obsessed with overpowering nature, with controlling and exploiting it. We take our pleasure in rapaciousness, and in rapacious tools like the Bulldozer. The Chain Saw. The Drilling Rig. The Continuous Miner. How could persons of goodwill, of sensitivity to nature — how could they reverse this evil juggernaut?

These ideas were not new to me; I used to preach them as artfully as the next fellow. But that afternoon I had profoundly conflicting thoughts as I listened to these old, familiar hymns. I *owned* a chain saw, and I could not imagine working up the pile of firewood I need to heat my house each winter without such an efficient implement of forest-rape. And the one tool I would have loved most of all to own was a bulldozer — imagine being able to climb on a machine and make all the rough places plain on my little farm! Imagine sculpting the whole landscape to suit my purpose! Then I thought: if someone told me I had a coal seam buried in my cliff, I might damn well wish I owned a continuous miner.

It had happened slowly, gradually, but I had become something more than a New Age ideologue. I had become a farmer. When nature and I were getting along well, I could grudgingly acknowledge that we shared a sort of partnership. But much of the time we were quarreling. And some of the time, nature was causing me a lot of grief.

Farmers have a saying: if you want to see it rain, make hay. Why is it so often true? Nature may be aptly perceived as a maternal force, but if any human mother matched her for austerity, I expect the state would imprison her for child abuse. Nature simply doesn't care. She is as apt to serve up a deluge as a sunny day, as apt to decimate a lamb crop with a late spring blizzard as to nurture growing things with moderate warmth and appropriate precipitation. She will make a desert of a meadow, and vice versa; behind even her most benign behavior lurk profound and unpredictable urges to chaos. Some mom. Some business partner.

The partnership seems to go one hell of a lot better when the human partners equip themselves with machines. Big ones. Strong ones. There's nothing like a snowplow, for example, to help sort out one's relationship with nature in the depths of winter. She can do what she wants to do, and you can do what you want to do, and over time it gets to be an almost pleasant tug-of-war. There's nothing like a screamingly high-powered, low-impedance fence charger spitting out five thousand volts on a bare wire when you want to appreciate the beauty of nature in the form of, say, a coyote. There's nothing like a $37,000 reverse-osmosis hyperfiltration rig to ease the partnership with nature when it comes to making maple syrup.

Machines, however, tend to take on lives of their own. They tend to become characters. They have a way of quitting on you at the darnedest times; and they seem to respond as well to being *talked to* properly as to being stroked with the right wrenches and lubricants. It's a dark plot, all right: machines tend to machinate.

So the owners of machines develop complicated feelings about them; this turns out, I think, to be a piece of luck for nature. Time and again, the machines do not so much help man rape nature as they serve to buffer his ambivalent relationship with her. As thunderheads loom above raked hay waiting to be baled, chances are the farmer is cursing his broken baler rather more loudly than the Source of Impending Rain. Chances are he is thumbing, with grease-blackened fingers, through some very thick and quite confusing operator's manual. "Needle Yoke Penetration." "Feeder Tine Timing." "Knotter Brake Torque Adjustment." Now, who is the farmer going to blame? He *knows* who made the baler.

In this way, I suggest that much of modern man's potential malevolence toward nature — that silent partner — is unwittingly diverted onto the backs of multinational corporations, which can bear it. It may not be the best arrangement, but better to kick a cold machine than the ineffable, if one has to kick something. Nature, seen from this perspective, has a good thing going with modern man, after all: she has got machines out there running interference for her. In the words of Archimedes, then, I say: Give me a lever.

• I Think That I Shall Never See

A neighboring farmer, a man who has little use for organized religion, likes to tell a joke about the minister who came to visit. "You and the Almighty," the man of God exclaimed, "have certainly produced a fine corn crop here!"

The farmer said nothing.

"You and the Almighty do a fine job with alfalfa!"

The farmer winced but kept his peace.

"You and the Almighty grew a lovely field of barley!"

"Hold it," said the farmer. "Just hold it right there. The Almighty farmed this place all by himself, once. Before my grandpa got here. And the Almighty wasn't growing any corn, or any alfalfa, or barley. All He could figure out how to grow was *trees.*"

"The Almighty loves a proud forest," agreed the minister.

"Grandpa *cleared* these fields of the Almighty's trees. And we've been fighting the Almighty to *keep* them clear ever since. So don't you hitch me up with Him — I've never seen the Almighty grow alfalfa in my life!"

A century ago, when Vermont had one million sheep, three-quarters of the state's forests had been cleared for grazing. Cleared by men working without benefit of chain saws, or bulldozers, or log skidders. Nowadays, less than one quarter of the state is open; millions of acres have reverted to a forested condition. Throughout rural New England, the story is the same, as though the Lord were indeed determined to grow trees here. Let a pasture go ungrazed, leave a meadow unmowed for a few short years, and the forest creeps back, silently regenerating itself. First come innocuous red cedars and sumacs, then white pines and spruces, and finally the northern hardwoods move in. Oak, maple, hickory, ash — once these get established in a neglected field, one can forget about farming it for the next fifty years.

Old-timers shake their heads and mutter imprecations against landowners so lazy and shortsighted as to let forests reclaim meadows. This is seen as a wanton waste of agricultural resources, a betrayal of our forebears who bequeathed us open land. As though it were a trust. But the sad truth is, much of Vermont today is bought and sold in parcels too small to farm with any hope of profit. So land goes neglected, and trees crop up overnight.

The first line of defense against encroaching forest is a mower; trees just cannot get established in a field where hay is annually cut. But after a year or three, baby trees develop woody stems that stop a hay mower dead. This is the stage at which a newly settled out-of-stater — just like I was once — realizes that cleared land does not *stay* cleared without regular attention. No matter what one paid for it. I had bought a farm, but it was poised to transform itself to forest right before my eyes.

The answer was a mowing machine of a different type: a Bush Hog. Bush Hogs are the heavy-duty, overgrown cousins of the common lawn mowers pushed around the backyards of suburbia. Coupled to a twenty-five-horsepower tractor, a Bush Hog mower can whack its way through baby trees as thick as a man's thumb. It may not leave a hay field in a state suitable for baling, but it will reverse the process of reforestation so that fields can grow hay again.

I obtained a Bush Hog, secondhand, from a farmer who believed he had worn it out; over the next couple of years I managed to abuse it mightily, asserting myself against colonizing trees and also against dozens of rocks and boulders hiding in the tall, rank grass. Anyone who mows a field several years running comes to pay a tuition in learning where the rocks are; I paid with that poor old Bush Hog, slapping its six-pound blades into hard, cold stone until it finally *was* worn out. For good. And since then, I have come to regard forests as the entropy to which nature, undirected, seems inclined. At least in these parts. I celebrate the Bush Hog as a way of beating nature down — and as a way of forcing her to grow more useful crops.

The New England forest — and particularly the scraggly, second-growth reforestation that occurs in neglected fields — is not exactly the forest primeval. But once it gets established beyond the avail of Bush Hogs, landowners customarily turn to chain saws to get a handle on things. Each autumn, for example, just as hordes of tourists invade Vermont to glimpse its gaudy foliage, an army of Vermonters enters the same forests with intent to fell perhaps a million trees for winter fuel. Standing timber is so ridiculously inexpensive — three to five dollars per cord is a common price — that even those who don't own woodlots can well afford to convert a few days' hard labor into a winter's warmth. On balance, such cutting of fuel wood as we see today probably improves the forest and can be a prudent means of keeping it under control.

The problem is, people all too like myself are apt to treat their woodlot as a garden in which weeds are never pulled. We only take the vegetables — that is, we have no time to harvest any but the best trees. The ugly trees, with misshapen trunks and countless stocky branches crawling out in every direction, will be left to grow forever. They are just too difficult to fell and work up into cordwood. And so, many forests just become uglier with each passing year.

Ugly forest or not, chain saw ownership conveyed to me a marvelous sense of power. More so than a Bush Hog, even. I began to feel as though any tree on the place was there by my *permission;* after all, I could in principle make it disappear. Visiting dear friends in Boston, I strode through the Public Garden and thought: These are not big trees. I could fell them all in a solid afternoon of work, then move on to reclaim the Common and return it to pasture.

Unfortunately, there is more to clearing land than merely dropping trees. For every tree dropped — and bucked up into firewood — there is a stump left poking from the ground. And pulling stumps makes felling trees look easy. It is, I decided quickly enough, work fit only for a bulldozer.

I do not own a bulldozer, though often I have dreamed of owning one. Could any tool give greater satisfaction to its owner? I clipped out, not long ago, a photograph of dozers in the Amazon jungle. They worked in pairs, these huge machines, dragging between them a massive chain which would fell many acres of trees in a single day. So much for *that* rain forest. Eco-catastrophe? Sure, I admit it. But I also secretly admit to myself: Wow! Those boys think big!

Even a teensy-weensy bulldozer would help me out, and make me feel I had a convincing edge on Mother Nature. But recently I met a Vermonter who thinks big, himself — fellow name of Gary Orvis. After years of hiring out to clear land with large bulldozers, this man got the fine idea to build a machine that could mow trees. *Trees*, not little shoots and saplings. He pulls the machine behind a Caterpillar D-7, a dozer of respectable size, and any tree the dozer can push over in one pass can be reduced to broomstick-size splinters in a flash. In practice, this amounts to eight- to ten-inch-diameter trees.

I went to see this new machine. It looked like a Bush Hog mower with true delusions of grandeur. Four blades — each weighing 110 pounds — whirled around a central axis at a tip speed of 168 miles per hour. The power source was a 187-horse-power diesel engine dedicated solely to turning those blades. Clever but simple shock-absorbing devices were built into the power train and thick steel shrouding of the mower's frame; when trees are being ground up into broomsticks, provision must be made for bumps and bounces.

"You *made* this?" I asked, dumbfounded. The machine weighed four tons.

"All by myself. Got the idea, see, and people said I couldn't do it. Said it wouldn't work. But I just kept thinking, there's a lot of fields growing up to trees out there. Lot of work around for a tool like this."

"How much did it cost you?"

"Oh, gosh, I don't know. I got the idea, see, then I just started collecting parts. Scrap steel here, old hydraulics there — it just sort of gradually came together. Spent a couple months last winter welding it all up. Folks around here call it my wet dream."

"But . . . it works?"

He grinned. "It works. I showed 'em."

"How fast can you pull the thing?"

"Oh, that all depends. Maybe three acres an hour, but I think I ought to run across a field twice. From two directions. Makes a finer splinter, so the wood rots down quicker."

I can seldom mow *hay* at three acres an hour. Why, with this man's machine, a flatlander could let his fields go to hell for fifteen years, then beat the forest back in no time. "Think of a big ax blade chopping at 168 miles an hour," he told me. The man spoke softly, but his voice was full of creative pride. "You could get a lot of wood cut."

I thought: I will have to hire that machine, one of these days. I have nine rough acres that are too far gone to Bush Hog back into pasture, and clearing them with a chain saw would require a summer's work. *Before* bulldozing the stumps. But I also thought: I can wait a few years, yet, and still have my emerging forest well within the range of this machine's capabilities. When eight-inch trees can be mowed down like clover, reforestation problems become less urgent.

There are some people, I realize, who feel that trees have an inherent and almost mystical value. More than one visitor has quoted Joyce Kilmer to me as I have cleaned and oiled my trusty chain saw. I myself recall growing up in South Jersey, where there were so few trees on the fifteen-mile route to Camden that one could almost *count* them. Then I, too, respected trees. But in Vermont, the Almighty wants to have his forest back, and anyone who wants to farm is locked in mortal combat. Once we give up felling trees, it won't be long before we can no longer see the forest for them.

• Ohm on the Range

There are many, many stories about electric fences, and nearly all of them lead to the same jolting punch line: somebody, somewhere got a whizzing shock. Why don't people take a clue from livestock and *learn?* Well, it isn't easy. When one lives with nice, hot fences — relying on them daily to keep farm animals inside and hungry predators outside of far-flung pastures — one becomes resigned to experiencing inadvertent electrification several times a year. Count on it. Each of these shocks can, sad to say, make a grown person sit right down and cry. And yet, crying, one remembers: we could scarcely farm New England without these painful, high-tech fences.

I can still recall my first encounter with a charged fence. It was on my great-uncle's dairy farm, in Wisconsin; I was six years old. "Don't you touch that wire, there," the good man warned my older sister and me. "See it, there? On insulators? That wire's live."

"What does *live* mean?" my sister asked.

"That means it's electric."

I thought, Holy cow! Right here in broad daylight? Waist-high? Why would someone do a thing like that?

"Keeps the cows clear out of the cornfield," drawled the old farmer.

Next day, my sister ran to show me half a dozen crows sitting on the same wire. Obviously, she declared, they were not getting shocked. Soon enough, I got into a classic double-dare situation. *Zap!* I ran howling up the lane, resolved to get the hell away from farms forever.

I did not keep this promise, though. And when, many years later, I found myself *becoming* a farmer, I was surprised to learn that laying out and building and maintaining fences is a mighty big, expensive, time-consuming part of a livestock farmer's work. Even relatively small farms can require several *miles* of perimeter and interior fencing; the investment for these can quickly run into thousands of dollars.

One of the precious few ways to lower the cost of fencing is to go electric. A couple strands of wire that can serve up a decent shock are worth half a dozen passive strands, and will even rival woven wire for containing animals. With a hot fence, wire gauge can be reduced — saving steel — and posts can be spaced much farther apart. Such a fence, while saving a bundle on materials and erection, can actually be more effective at deterring predators than conventional types; more than one farmer, having shelled out for a five-foot-high woven and barbed-wire fence, has been confounded to see dogs or coyotes scramble right over it. When a much simpler fence is charged good and hot, however, animals won't mess with it.

My initial fencing problem, when I moved to Vermont, was to keep the neighbor's heifers out of my half-finished house and off my car; the owner of these fun-loving bovines showed me how to stretch a single strand of barbed wire between skinny, self-insulating fiberglass wands. Then he directed me to a farm store where I obtained a battery-operated "fencer," or charging unit. This was an old-fashioned, coil-and-breaker-point type of charger, no doubt similar to the one my great-uncle in Wisconsin had owned some thirty years before. It spat out a few milliamps of current at about one thousand volts for a healthy fraction of each second; this quickly won the heifers' respect, without positively frying unwary humans. It delivered capably the well-defined, invigorating sting that rural folks know all too well. In retrospect, though, it was a primitive machine.

Seeing my first electric fence newly erected, a local youth then in the throes of adolescent dissipation dropped by to test it for me.

"What do you mean, test it?" I demanded.

"Hey, there's not a charger made that I can't grab the fence. And hang right on to it. Show you?"

"Well, that fence shocks heifers pretty good."

"It don't make no nevermind."

Even in those early days, I realized that rural living offered young men many novel tests of masculinity. And here was one. It smacked, in a down-home way, of getting high — or at least of shaking off the befuddlement of hangover. I shrugged. "I'm not going to stop you."

The young man walked over and grabbed hold of my fence. And grimaced. "Hey," he asked, twitching ever so slightly, "whose make of charger *is* this?"

"It's a Bull-Dozer."

"Got a nice . . . *tingle* . . . to it." He let go, after what must have been a good half-dozen shocks. "Not bad. That should be a good one."

He climbed into his unmuffled car and roared away; as soon as he had left, I tiptoed over and tried my fence. And ran howling back into the house. Suckered? Well, not exactly. But I had a lot to learn.

A fence charger throws a pulse of current out onto a fence, but no circuit exists until someone or something connects that current to the ground. The quality of ground connection largely determines the amount of shock a victim feels; for example, extremely droughty soils can be such poor conductors that the average fence charge is rendered ineffective. Likewise, a sheep in full, dry fleece is surrounded by a fine electrical insulator. And, in the case of my fence-testing youth, sneakers with thick rubber soles can substantially reduce the amount of current passing through one's feet into the ground. I, on the other hand, had tested my fence in open-toed sandals. Virtually barefoot.

As time went by, I learned other circumstances under which my fence would fail to serve its purpose. Weeds growing high enough to touch the charged wire could wick away a good portion of its sting, particularly when wet with dew or soaked with rain. Such constant leakage of current quickly sapped the battery that ran my charger; when the fence lost power, frisky heifers would galumph right through it. Electric fences, usually, do not constitute a strong *mechanical* barrier to the forward progress of grazing cattle. Without a good shock, they are nothing. Heifers are apt to make you prove it to them every day.

Finally, my old charger had a design problem common to units of its type. It is one thing to serve up a sting that victims will remember; it is something else again to do so without killing them dead. An idle fear? I thought so, till the day I saw my two-year-old son jerk about spasmodically, one hand seemingly glued to the electric fence. I ran to pry him off, and held him for a good ten minutes before he regained his metabolic composure.

Investigating what had caused this near-tragic accident, I learned that coil-and-breaker-point fence chargers have a relatively long pulse duration — two-tenths of a second, say. When a good shock rips through one's muscles, they contract; brushing an electric fence with an open palm, one's entire hand may be forced to grab the wire involuntarily when the current is delivered. The "off" cycle — three-quarters of a second, say — may not be long enough to extricate one's hand from the fence before the next shock ripples down the line.

Such repeated shocking, in surprisingly little time, can lead to heart arrhythmia and death.

This episode caused me to approach electric fencing with a

newfound sense of caution. By now I was raising quite a few sheep, though, and I had erected several thousand feet of new electric fences; I could not turn back. Fortunately, not long after my son's electrification, I read about remarkable new fence "energisers" recently developed in New Zealand and Australia, and now being imported here. Expensive. Awesomely powerful, yet much safer than old-fashioned fencers. Triumphs of British expatriate inventiveness.

I bought one. A plug-in model — no more batteries to charge. Furthermore, it had solid-state electronics. No moving parts. Instead of a measly one-thousand-volt current, this machine could theoretically deliver *seven times* that much; even under adverse conditions — wet weeds, dry ground, sneakers — this "energiser" could lay down a screaming shock. But its pulse *duration* had been whittled down to the merest 3/10,000 of a second, with the balance of each second in the "off" cycle. In short, this machine produced an unforgettable sting, but an extremely brief and therefore safe one.

The neighborhood fence tester, naturally, came to try it. Wearing his protective footgear. I still like to recall his hand flying off the wire at a hundred miles an hour. Before his face reacted, even. "Wow!" he yelped. "That's *something!*" He shook his arm, smarting. "That's a whole new ball game."

And it was, indeed. Fifty yards away, inside my house, the radio began to go pop-pop-pop in time with the charger. Even the *car* radio, driving down the road. The problem, I was led to believe, involved inadequate grounding of the fancy charger; but adequate grounding — at least on the alluvial soils I had to work with — would have required virtually building another fence, underground, to complete the circuit effectively.

Stray voltage started showing up in the darnedest places. I had an electrically heated, automatic watering bowl in the barn, and I couldn't understand how come the sheep had lost interest in it. They *seemed* to be thirsty, but I couldn't get them near the thing. Finally I squatted down and nosed it, sheeplike, for a drink — and got knocked right on my ass. Pop-pop-pop.

I decided I had bought more charger than my farm could really handle, so I traded down to a reasonably modern, low-impedance unit that was somewhat less aggressive about doing its job. Three thousand volts on a fence, I have come to feel, is all I really need.

And even that is too much, sometimes. A drawback of total commitment to electric fences is that every single lamb must be trained to respect them in a carefully staged seminar; you can't just turn them out to hit the fence full tilt as part of some carefree gambol. Why is this? I learned the hard way, when a lamb, who was perhaps not the brightest lamb I've ever seen, managed to get himself completely tangled up. Completely. And he was vividly energized.

I saw it from a distance and ran to free him from the fence, but I found *myself* energized, too, the moment I touched him. So I sprinted back into the barn to shut the charger off; but by the time I came back out, the poor lamb had expired.

Bummer — but a farmer does not disdain to convert such mishaps into meat for his table. I skinned and gutted the unfortunate lamb, and brought the little carcass to my wife for cooking. The result was nothing short of astounding. Gourmets take note: electrocuted baby lamb is simply the most tender, the juiciest meat that I have ever experienced. Like eating butter. Melts right in your mouth — you don't need teeth, even.

There might be some market for this product, though I am not low enough to try to find it. But I ask: who knows where rural electrification will ultimately lead? Who knows what new uses are waiting to be found for nice, hot fences?

• Baleology

There are times in a Yankee farmer's year when half a dozen important tasks demand a person's simultaneous attention. Not so in June, however. In June, one crucial chore simply has no peer: mowing and raking and baling hay in a timely and efficient fashion. Profitably operating a farm throughout the balance of the year can depend, very largely, on the successful production of this first cutting of hay.

Modern technologies for making hay are emblematic of the changes wrought in Western agriculture over the past fifty years. There are men alive — and farming — in my corner of Vermont who remember mowing hay with scythes, raking it with wooden rakes, and piling it up into picturesque haystacks such as Monet delighted to depict on canvas. That is how human beings made hay on this planet for — well, for millennia; but in our lifetime, such methods have continued only in the Third World. In New England today, haying is anything but peasant work.

Our county fair, which is big on nostalgia, continues to sponsor a hand-mowing contest. It gives the old-timers reason to keep their scythes and muscles keen, and some can still mow at a rate that would translate into an acre in a long day's work. But the standard tool for mowing the county's farm meadows today is the New Holland Model 489 Haybine, which knocks down a nine-foot swath at speeds well over five miles an hour. And that's not all. It does *more* than knock hay down: it sends it flying through huge rollers, similar to those on a clothes wringer, where intermeshing rubber chevrons crush and crimp the stems of the plants to speed up their drying time, and it spits the mown hay out into high, fluffy, preformed windrows. In an eight-hour working day, such a machine can mow fifty acres of hay — or what, only yesterday, half a dozen hard-working paisans might have hoped to mow in a solid week.

The man wielding a scythe does not have a substantial investment in his mowing tool. Unfortunately, today's New Holland Model 489 Haybine lists for $10,299, and it takes at least a $12,000 tractor to pull the thing across a meadow. We have sought — and won — fantastic labor productivity, but it certainly has not come cheap. And, as mowing machines go, the Model 489 is not a truly high-capacity one. For considerably steeper prices we can buy machines capable of mowing *ten* acres per hour. Even in a June full of stormy, unsettled weather, such machines can put up an awful lot of hay.

The widespread use of haying machines of such awesome capabilities can pose real dilemmas for smaller, part-time farmers like myself. First, we can't afford them. We would have to mow a couple of hundred acres several times a year before the cost of a Model 489 would start to look reasonable. We would have to make, say, twenty thousand bales of hay a year. At two thousand bales per year — *my* kind of scale — owning the mower would cost more than the hay is worth.

Second, although I know that owning a Model 489 Haybine would be a powerful confirmation of my masculinity, I have enough trouble creating the illusion that I *work* here on the farm *without* having my mowing time on thirty acres of hay reduced to a scant five hours. Getting the whole farm mowed before lunchtime on a single June morning would add many quiet hours to my summer schedule — hours that my wife and others might mistake for idleness. So the breakneck pace set by my neighbors' powerful machines is simply not for me.

Third, the plain truth is that I borrowed a neighbor's Model 489 Haybine, and his ninety-horsepower tractor, to mow one of my fields a few years ago. Running such a huge, expensive, whining rig scared the living daylights out of me.

So I mow hay with a machine of intermediate technology, whose proper name is the Avco-New Ideal Model 272 Cut-Ditioner. It cost only a couple of thousand bucks, used. Basically, the machine turns heavy, swinging steel flails that whack the dickens out of grass or whatever else they may encounter. Frogs, snakes, field mice, medium-size rocks all get spewed out by my mower in a state of concussion suitable for baling. Sixty-five horsepower, I think, would adequately power this ingenious machine; but since my biggest tractor only puts out forty horses, I have to wade through my fields of waving hay at speeds under two miles per hour. Under *one* mile per hour, sometimes. At these speeds, merely staying awake can get to be a problem.

With the benefit of historical perspective, I remind myself that 99.9 percent of haymakers who ever mowed the earth's green pastures would be astounded to see me mowing hay at the phenomenal rate of an acre in a single hour. The bad news is that the other .1 percent of haymakers are all my contemporaries, and they are all mowing hay at several times my plodding rate. Frankly, I find it emasculating to watch a neighbor felling fifty acres in the time it takes me to mow five. I am only a fraction as productive as the next fellow; is my time really only a fraction as valuable?

Others in my situation have opted to own the high-capacity machines, purchasing them used from big-time haymakers. But such mowers and balers have problems of their own. An all-out custom-haying operation can run a machine till it is virtually worn out even before the paint begins to fade. Such bargains are akin to two-year-old cars with 120,000 miles on them; they look sharp, but the price just can't be right enough.

I know a man, a part-time farmer like myself, who purchased

a used hay baler that fit into this category of almost-new-but-very-used equipment. Now, the hay baler is a remarkable machine, a cross between a fine Swiss watch and a Rube Goldberg contraption. Scores of moving steel fingers lift hay gently off the ground and pass it to an auger. The auger hands it to a giant plunger that packs it into an endless sausage of regular shape and uniform density. Every now and then, the baler wraps a piece of that sausage in sisal twine and ties it off. Incredible. The power source for all this intricate activity comes from a strong tractor's power-takeoff shaft; but to even out the plunger's intermittent thrusts, a substantial flywheel has to whirl between the tractor's power output and the baler's power intake. Substantial — like 295 pounds and twenty-seven inches in diameter. Revolving several hundred times per minute, such a flywheel represents a huge reservoir of energy.

I know a man, a part-time farmer like myself, who turned around while baling with his newish-but-used baler just in time to see its flywheel separate from the machine. Several bolts broke, a heavy gland nut was reduced to filings, and the flywheel took off across his field. Stunned, the driver stopped baling to watch. The flywheel rolled right through a woven-wire fence one hundred yards away, then through a barnyard gate — and through the barn itself — without stopping. In one wall and out the other. Much later, the farmer found the flywheel had come to rest against an oak tree in his woodlot.

"Right through the *barn?*" I repeated, not quite believing what I'd heard.

"Objects in motion," he said dryly, "tend to stay in motion."

He had to revise his wear estimate on that baler.

One of the more problematic issues posed by hay balers centers on what happens to the bales when they reach the baler's end. At first, no doubt, farmers were delighted simply to have the things fall on the ground. Compared with loading hay onto wagons with a pitchfork, picking up neatly tied bales must have seemed a picnic. It is not the way of modern agriculture, though, to be satisfied for long with such an unmechanized state of affairs.

The simplest answer was to hitch a flatbed wagon to the rear of the baler and to station a man on the wagon to pull bales from the bale chute and stack them, pending transport to the barn. But the modern farmer would rather pay a lot of men to build machines in grimy factories — a practice he supports each time he buys a machine — than pay one man to ride around on his hay wagon in the fresh air. So it wasn't long before the "kicker" was invented.

The kicker is a machine that attaches to the rear end of a hay baler and automatically sends bales flying through the air into the very large basket of a high-sided wagon. One such wagon — sixteen feet long, eight feet wide, and ten to twelve feet high — can hold about one hundred bales deposited in the random fashion kickers are known for. A modern high-capacity baler fills such a wagon in a matter of minutes, so today's farmer has to have quite a fleet of them. Each wagon costs one thousand dollars, more or less, but that is small potatoes. The baler itself goes for ten thousand dollars, the kicker for three thousand dollars more. And — as in mowing — it takes twelve thousand dollars worth of tractor, minimum, to haul this unlikely train.

There are two main types of kickers. The first, called a bale thrower, relies on two rubber flat-belts moving at high speed to squeeze each bale and shoot it out, like a watermelon seed between two fingers. This is the old way, and it has certain drawbacks. The *new* way to kick bales is with John Deere's Hydra-Load Bale Ejector. *Ejector* is the word, all right. The freshly made bale drops onto a throwing pan, a lever trips, and a powerful hydraulic pump launches the bale skyward. With proper adjustment, the bale follows a high parabolic trajectory and ends up in the moving wagon.

There are other maneuvers this contrivance can perform, attesting to the sophisticated engineering for which John Deere is famous. On a sidehill, a remote hydraulic cylinder can tilt the ejector to compensate for slope. From the tractor seat the operator punches buttons on a control panel to adjust throwing force in order to fill his wagons thoroughly from front to back. With experience and skill, even eighty-pound bales can be vaulted to the top rear of a high-sided hay wagon.

I know a man, a part-time farmer like myself, who bought a used Hydra-Load Bale Ejector to kick hay into his wagons. Trouble was, he didn't get the control box at the tractor seat wired properly to the hydraulic pump at the business end of the machine. In fact, it wasn't wired up at all. It only *seemed* to be. On the first day he tried out the new toy, he found himself making not eighty-pound bales but thirty-pound bales. And the ejector, unbridled from its controls, was kicking at maximum force.

Imagine this citizen-farmer turning around to watch his kicker spring into action, only to see the first bale sent flying thirty feet skyward. It landed a surprising distance *behind* the wagon, on the freshly mowed ground. The operator shut down the tractor, climbed off, and jogged the length of the twenty-foot-long baler, the six-foot-long ejector, the sixteen-foot-long wagon, plus another twenty-four feet to where the bale lay. He picked it up, ran it back to the high-sided wagon, and heaved with all his strength to toss it in.

Back on the tractor, he punched the control box several times to reduce kicking force, but on the very next bale the same thing happened. And happened again. And the next time, too. In fact, no matter how many times he punched the little button, that kicker seemed determined to launch each bale into orbit. It got to where the operator was regarding his fine machine with utter fear and loathing: "Oh, no; oh, no, it's made a bale again, it's going to — oh, *no!*" This is not the kind of attitude toward a Hydra-Load Ejector that John Deere likes to foster in its patrons.

After filling one hay wagon under extreme constraints — the hardest sort of haying modern man might ever hope to suffer — he staggered home and flopped down with the owner's manual. Next day, he found the glitch in his ejector's circuitry. And now he is, against all odds, a satisfied customer. A professor, he says, of the science of baleology.

No doubt there are further technological advances heading down the pike — haymaking tools that will make today's state-of-the-art mowers and balers look like scythes and pitchforks. At the rate we're going, it may not be long before this entire county needs only a single mower — very wide, very quick — and a single very-high-capacity baler to put up all our hay in a few hot June days. Then men will wax sentimental about the good old days, when thousands of men on thousands of tractors sallied forth to mow green meadows. Still, today's pioneers of high-tech are closer to that one man who will bale up the whole county than they are to the scythe-wielding peasants of yesteryear. He, like they, will look on haying as a struggle with machinery more than with nature. And he, like they, will be working for the bank.

• Capital-Intensive Syrup

The standard maple syrup can still depicts a sap-gatherer trudging through snowdrifts toward the distant sugarhouse, sap pails dangling from his shoulder yoke; but it is a brave new world out there in the sugarbush, and men whose work is carrying pails are now an endangered species. In the modern maple orchard, they have been replaced by plumbing. Entire hillside forests have now been catheterized, with five-sixteenths-inch plastic tubing draining sap from tapholes into pipes of progressively larger diameter, until a fat plastic artery dumps the stuff out into a holding tank next to the evaporator. Look, Ma — no buckets!

A typical sugarbush of two thousand taps — producing, in a good year, some four hundred gallons of syrup — requires roughly *six miles* of tubing to plumb. Thousands of dollars. In the early systems, all this tubing had to be taken down and cleaned each spring, after sugaring season; now, though, it is flushed in place and left strung through the woods year-round. The sugarer has become, above all else, a plumber.

Economics forced the change. For decades, a rule of thumb was that a sap-gatherer's daily wage should be about the price of a gallon of syrup; but syrup prices could not keep pace, in modern times, with increases in even the minimum wage. Then came the energy crunch, and all the progressive sugarmakers who had quietly switched from wood-fired boiling to oil-fired boiling found themselves in deep trouble. It can take better than four gallons of fuel oil to produce the heat needed to make one gallon of syrup.

Tubing bought some time for a declining syrup industry — by putting a lot of sap-gatherers out of work — but it was just the first stage in an ongoing revolution. Once those forests had been intubated at no small expense, someone got the bright idea to *suck* sap from the maple trees rather than just letting it drip, drip, drip from tapholes. Suck it with a vacuum pump, just like dairymen suck milk from cows. Sure enough, vacuum extraction about doubled the sap that could be coaxed from trees.

I went to see a sugarmaker/plumber — the new breed — who had invested substantially in these technologies, and walked through his sugarbush to see what could go wrong. A lot of things could, he told me. "Sugar season — that's right when we're apt to get wet snow. Or windstorms. If a tree branch falls onto the pipeline, let alone a tree, you can lose a lot of sap before you figure something's wrong."

"What about freezing?"

"If you set the runs up right — always downhill, always sloping like they should — it's not supposed to freeze. And the new tubing can be stretched real tight. But if you get a sag, and freezing — well, you know sap can turn to snot mighty quickly."

I said I hadn't known that.

"It's from the enzymes. Once you get sap from a tree, you don't want to let it set. You want to get it boiled."

"How much time do you have to spend checking up on plumbing?"

"Couple of weeks, anyway. Before we start sugaring. Then I'll walk the lines after every sap run, every storm — but it's no work at all compared to hauling pails. The worst damage seems to come from squirrels, mice — rodent mischief. Either they just like to chew, or tubing's got some salt or something in it that they like. They make us cut and splice a lot of tubing every year. All in all, though, it works pretty darn slick. And we're drawing sap from trees that gatherers could never get to."

I asked to see the man's sugarhouse next, but he warned me it was far from state of the art. In fact, the whole wood-fired evaporator was in a state of major overhaul, because under full boil a mouse had managed to drown in the holding tank and plug up the orifice draining sap into the pans where it is changed to syrup. Things can happen fast when an evaporator burns wood at the rate of several cords per day; without adequate sap in the pans to absorb that heat, something akin to a nuclear core meltdown takes place. The solder in the pans melts, leaving a sickening and expensive mess.

I recalled hearing that a market for maple sap — unboiled — had developed in certain areas of Vermont. Half a dozen sugar-makers would give up evaporating on their own farms, and merely collect sap to sell to a boiling operation of truly efficient size. So, staring at a couple of thousand dollars' worth of pans that had tried to self-destruct, I asked: "Why don't you just run sap from your pipeline into a tank truck, and haul it to someone else?"

"Because," he said, "it costs me fourteen cents a gallon to get sap down to this end of the pipeline. And sap sells for twelve cents a gallon — *after* trucking it."

This struck me as a compelling argument. But if a sugarmaker, even a modern sugarmaker/plumber, could scarcely get his own sap to the sugarhouse at the price he could buy somebody else's sap for, then something was surely amiss in the sugar business. "You mean," I asked, "all the profits come from boiling down?"

The mere mention of profits caused his mouth to twist into a rueful smile. Forty gallons of sap, he recited, to make a gallon of maple syrup. Five to six dollars worth of sap, that came to. Energy costs in the neighborhood of four dollars per gallon of syrup produced. Amortization of a sugarhouse, evaporator, and sundry capital investment running well into five figures. Even the gallon cans for retail syrup — the ones with the pretty scene of busy sap-gatherers — cost producers a buck and a half each.

"But some folks," I protested, "must have found a way to make syrup pay."

"What you want to see," he told me, "is my neighbor's operation. He's gone to reverse osmosis."

"Come again?"

Rather than explain, he packed me in his pickup truck and took me to his neighbor's place. Much bigger operation. And there, running the full length of the back wall in the sugarhouse, was a $37,000 reverse-osmosis machine. Simply, a ten-horsepower pump squeezed water out of sap by pressing it through a cellulose acetate filter, a filter fine enough to discriminate between molecules of water and those of sugar. In consequence, one thousand gallons of two percent sugar sap could be reduced in an hour's time to three hundred thirty-three gallons of six percent sugar concentrate. And that could be run through again to make a couple hundred gallons of ten percent sugar concentrate — *all without heat*. Then, with four-fifths of the water removed by this hyperfiltration, the balance could be boiled down to make maple syrup of acceptable flavor and color. Syrup is nominally sixty-four percent sugar.

"How long does it take a guy to pay for that machine?" I asked its proud owner.

"Well, mine's paid for. And it's only four years old. And I only *use* it two hundred hours a year."

"That's some payback," I said.

"That's just fuel savings — I had quite a little oil bill before I bought that thing. And I *still* do. But it's down to one dollar of oil per gallon of syrup, and that's a good deal."

"How come everybody hasn't got one of these machines?"

"Everybody hasn't got thirty-seven thousand dollars sitting in his piggy bank. And farmers — most farmers — are already borrowed to their limit."

So, for those who can afford it, there is more than one way to convert maple sap to syrup. In fact, pretty soon the man was telling me a third way: boiling under vacuum. Just as one can boil water high in the Rocky Mountains at less than 212 degrees — because altitude diminishes the atmospheric pressure — it turns out that sap will boil at 135 degrees under a vacuum of twenty inches of mercury. And that, too, results in dramatic fuel savings.

Boiling, whether under vacuum or not, is bound to produce tremendous quantities of waste heat, and plenty of new devices to recycle this resource are coming onto the market for high-tech sugarmakers. Modern evaporators are hooded affairs, channeling steam to where it can be used to preheat sap before it goes into the boiling pans; this technology is particularly important in operations that have gone to reverse osmosis, since the hyperfiltration membranes function most efficiently when sap is at fifty-five degrees, substantially warmer than it is apt to be when it arrives at the sugarhouse from a mountain pipeline. On the other hand, sap at fifty-five degrees is notoriously susceptible to spoilage from bacteria and yeasts. This has led to the use of ultraviolet light and other means to extend the shelf life of sap waiting to be boiled — one marvelous invention seems to require two or three more to sustain it, in an endless chain.

When the right technologies are coupled to the right-size sugarbush, however, maple syrup production once again becomes theoretically profitable. A labor of more than love. Those who would not want to do without the stuff on pancakes — and who doesn't wince at farm prices of roughly twenty dollars per gallon? — can be assured that hardy Vermonters will keep tapping maples. What will not be advertised, though, are the startling changes in how syrup is now made: the hardy Vermonters like to help customers think of them as yeomen toting wooden buckets through March snowdrifts, rather than as foremen in what amount to little chemical plants, keeping watch over phenomenally capital-intensive processes that minimize human labor and heat production.

The mythology of syrup must remain . . . well, syrupy. But

those who work to make the syrup need to nourish sweet dreams, too. Taking my leave of the reverse-osmosis sugarmaker, I didn't need to ask him if there was a dollar in it. He seemed as content as if he'd been told money grows on trees. Sugar maples. All around him. I expect they're going to be there — growing — for a long, long time.

• Shoveleers

Years ago, as my first Vermont winter bore down upon my consciousness, people started asking what I planned to do with snow. I answered cheerfully that I planned to enjoy it — skiing, sledding, even building the odd igloo. Soon enough I learned that I had misunderstood the question. The question was: what did I plan to do with the problem of snow *removal?* In these parts, it is a universal problem, and one that helps bind the human community together.

I didn't have the foggiest idea how I'd deal with snow removal. I guess I thought that I could pack the stuff down, or melt it, just by driving my car back and forth over it with sufficient vigor; that had worked well enough in southeastern Pennsylvania. For this more severe climate, I expected I might have to invest in studded snow tires. Maybe an aluminum snow shovel, even.

Neighbors shook their heads. For them, owning a highly mechanized, extremely heavy-duty, utterly reliable system for snow removal was just another necessity of life. Expensive, yes, but without a way to beat back winter, winter had a way of becoming intolerable. Winter was quite capable of bringing the unequipped life to a helpless standstill.

Not only did everyone around me make this urgent case; everyone around me had his house situated within fifty feet of the town road, which the town, of course, was responsible for keeping plowed. These folks had short driveways, and they had them for a reason, and they *still* had unbelievable snow removal implements. I, on the other hand, was living in a hay barn two hundred feet back from the road. My long-range plan was to build a dwelling *eight* hundred feet from it. But this is an old story: all the best building sites proximate to the road were seized years ago. So newcomers site their houses inland, and create long driveways.

Believe it or not, I did slog through my first Vermont winter with a set of studded snow tires and an aluminum shovel. But it was not a bit like southeastern Pennsylvania. We could get pasted two and three times in a single week, here; in between storms, gusty winds could drift the roads and driveways shut in just a few hours of rearranging the mountainous piles of snow that plows inevitably built up on the shoulders. There were days when I could shovel the driveway, zip into town for a couple of hours, and come home to an impassable situation — and it wasn't even snowing!

Naturally, I began to study my neighbors' tools and even to covet them, on the sly. By far the most popular device for attacking winter turned out to be a four-wheel-drive pickup truck — or Jeep, or Bronco, or Scout — with a six-foot Fisher All-Angle plow mounted ahead of the front bumper and controlled by a hydraulic pump driven by the engine. Vehicles so equipped were like knights of the rural highway. Within moments after a blizzard subsided, they were out in droves — dressing up the roads, opening sealed drives, and rescuing the stranded. They set things right, as though bound by some chivalrous code.

Then, too, their beefy plows often seemed like lances poised to joust with any stray or challenging object: mailboxes, guardrails, fenders of oncoming cars. The trucks, I had to guess, could *take* it. They could handle punishment. And the chevaliers spurring on these semiarmored vehicles looked unbowed, indefatigable — but when I went out to price the sort of rigs they all were driving, I quickly realized that their liege lord was the bank. Four-wheel drive can add a couple of thousand dollars to the price tag on a pickup truck, and a hydraulic plow can add a couple of thousand more. Furthermore, a wise man told me plowing snow can bring a pickup to an early demise: leaning all that traction and horsepower against the odd immovable object — such as, even, a frozen snowbank — can bend a truck's frame and compromise its handling traits permanently.

The snow knights were happy to offer me a free tow, in a jam, and one or two of them even volunteered to clear my driveway for me — once. Then they would suggest that I contract with them for snow removal, at fees ranging from twenty to forty bucks per shot. Vassalage, no doubt. I would just smile, wave my little shovel, and decline. If I paid myself that much each time I pushed the snow around, pretty soon I could afford some major-league snow tools of my own.

The second most popular snow-removal device turned out to be so-called lawn-and-garden tractors — those dinky toys for suburban estates — equipped with chains and wheel weights and front-mounted snowblowers. Assuming that one had one of these oversize riding lawn mowers, one could spend another thousand dollars to equip it to eat a drift approximately three feet wide and one foot high. This was not an overwhelming capacity, but snowblowers did have the distinct advantage of heaving snow a healthy distance from one's driveway, where it was less likely to come back to haunt one.

I was aspiring to a pickup-truck persona, however, not a lawn-and-garden style. All I lacked was the money. But then I saw that a lot of farmers managed to handle snow with a rear blade mounted on their tractors. Such blades were ordinarily used to scrape manure into a gutter in a barn floor, or perhaps to do mild field grading; to look at one, it was hard to visualize it plowing snow. The tractor, after all, had to drive *through* the entire snow drift before the plow ever had a chance to handle it. But snow is quite compressible, and even wet snow is never so dense as fresh manure or soil. By setting the rear blade at an oblique angle to the tractor's forward motion, fair amounts of snow could be gradually shuffled to one side.

Before my second winter, I had acquired a 1952 Ford tractor such as farmers were proud to own in 1952. Not a big tractor, but it had seriousness of purpose written all over it. It fit my newfound agricultural identity to a T; in fact, my identity drew strength in troubled moments just by climbing onto that machine and starting up the engine. And when snow began to fly, I shopped for a used rear blade and picked one up for a mere one hundred dollars, an astonishingly shrewd deal.

The matching of implements to tractors is a science, however. People go to ag schools to try to gain such expertise. I brought home a rear blade designed for, let us say, a 1962 tractor. When I mounted it to the three-point hitch on the rear end of my old Ford, the business end of any tractor, it looked mighty oversize. And when I raised the hydraulic lift lever to pick it up, I was surprised to watch the *front* end of the tractor levitate itself instead. The rear axle was a fulcrum, and I had attached more weight behind it than the engine and chassis represented up front.

I solved this teeter-totter problem with makeshift wheel weights on the front axle, and promptly blew a pressure safety-relief valve deep in the guts of the tractor's hydraulic system. Then I did what amateur farmers do all too often, trying to assemble the right team of mechanical servants: I bought a newer, bigger tractor so that I could pick up that one-hundred-dollar blade. The tractor was no bargain, but by now it's all water — or melted snow — over the dam.

At any rate, with patience and a little bit of forethought, a person can keep a driveway of short-to-intermediate length passable throughout even severe Vermont winters with a rear blade on a tractor. It takes patience because the tool is slow. It takes forethought because snow from the season's first storms needs to be trundled quite some distance downhill from where one would like to drive in midwinter. Otherwise, one quickly builds up snowbanks on each side of the right-of-way into which no more snow can be shunted. These banks turn to ice, and sit around for months; at a tractor's plodding speed, a rear blade just has no lifting force.

Long before I built a new house at the end of an eight-hundred-foot driveway, I began eyeing tractor-mounted snow-blowers. *Big* ones, not the lawn-and-garden type. I saw them clearing runways of snowbound airports, and I saw them in rural Quebec on the way to Montreal. These machines could move mountains, once a person got adept at driving in reverse. And since the tool mounted backwards, at least it always got to the snow before the tires did.

When I priced a stripped-down version of this implement, I was saddened but not surprised to learn it cost two thousand dollars. Big bucks, compared to a hundred-dollar blade. Things were worse than that, though: I took an ag-school course in farm management and learned how to quantify the true costs of such a tool. It involved depreciation schedules, useful life assumptions, opportunity costs of investment capital, and much more. Hitched to my tractor and including *its* running costs, every time I cleared the driveway with such a dazzling tool it was going to cost me seventy-two dollars. Plus my labor.

I filed that information, and life went on for several more years. Then, smack in the middle of haying season, in *June*, I picked up a farm paper on the sheerest intuition and there was an ad for a used tractor-mounted snowblower. Six-foot cut, three-foot height, eight hundred fifty pounds. Forty-horsepower tractor input. Excellent condition. And the asking price was just two hundred dollars.

I sprinted to the nearest phone. The guy selling a snowblower in June really wants to sell it — that much, I understood. But a price so low — had he slipped a zero? — was apt to bring buyers out of the hills.

The farm paper was ten days old; by amazing luck, though, when I called the seller he had just arrived back from vacation. "Had a few calls," he said. "Someone's coming here to see that machine right after supper."

I pulled out a map. It was after four P.M., and I was at least a ninety-minute drive away. "You mind if I leave right now?" I asked.

"Hell, no. Thing's not sold until it's sold. You show up here first, it's yours."

So I jumped into my truck and sped over several mountains, and, sure enough, there was the snow removal implement of my wildest dreams. Old, but — like he advertised — mint. I quickly made it mine.

Nowadays, I almost relish seeing the white stuff fall. I have the eight-hundred-foot driveway — a daunting distance — but I can *whoosh* it clear of anything in twenty minutes, commanding a machine that others nod to with respect. When a person sets his sights high at being a shoveleer, all things are possible.

Recently, however, I happened to see a snowplow rig that I would rather own. It was at the airport up here where I first admired a tractor-mounted snowblower; after a twenty-inch drop of lightweight, powder snow, a National Guard helicopter was dispatched to make the stuff go elsewhere. While the chopper hovered above the tarmac by a scant few feet, its tremendous downdraft would lift the snowdrifts upward. Then the wind would blow them off the runway.

My wife admired the ingenuity of this technique, but still tried to discourage me. After all, two-hundred-dollar helicopters are *really* scarce. "He blows snow, and you blow snow," she pointed out sagely. "It's a little different, sure, but what can he do that you can't?"

"Fly south, if he wants," I said. The ultimate revenge on winter.

• Use It Up

You can tell when it's been a good year on the farm: all the farmers are buying new pickup trucks. An unfortunate corollary is that in the absence of good years old trucks are kept running in advanced states of deterioration. Now and again one may actually croak and require replacement, ready or not; but the median age of pickups remains, in a state like Vermont, a leading indicator of agricultural prosperity.

My farm almost never has a good year — thanks to shrewd design — but our capital needs are also modest because we invoke an old-fashioned precept: use it up, wear it out, make it do or do without. This attitude predates Investment Tax Credits and Accelerated Cost Recovery Systems, but has not gone wholly out of favor. Last spring, though, even I had to make the painful admission that my truck was worn out.

I had driven the truck for eleven years; rust had made deep inroads into its structural integrity. I blamed an absent third party, a rustproofer who had charged a fine sum to protect my truck but then went bankrupt, defaulting on warranties. But I also blamed myself. For eleven years I had driven this truck without even once hosing it down, much less properly washing it. That was God's work, I used to think; but the truck contained numerous nooks and crannies that God never managed to reach. These corroded.

Asked how long I expected to drive the thing, I at first liked to say, "Forever." There *is* a farmer in these parts, a fellow after my own heart, whose 1954 Chevy is named Proud Tradition, the letters neatly painted across the tailgate. But forever is a long, long time; when my truck began to look visibly cancered, I changed my answer. I said I would drive it only until it fell apart.

Now, I did not mean this literally. But odd bits of steel began falling off my truck in earnest last winter, and then in March the door on the passenger side became unlatchable. This sounds insignificant, but it was a warning; don't two frayed shoelaces tend to break within days of each other? I drove onward, into April — slaloming through muddy ruts and bouncing over washboard gravel — and one day, on a stretch of especially punishing corduroy, the door on the driver's side of my truck slouched and broke off its hinges.

This door was not, I confess, a monolithic piece of steel. It had been some years since it had properly *thunked* on being slammed; in fact, it was now slathered with brown and blue-green Bondo, which I had casually molded around wads of steel wool stuffed into the general vicinity of where the bottom of the door had been. It was not an expert body job, but a better one than I had done on the floorboards when a routine inspection revealed them to have disappeared.

I think we lack, here in Vermont, a truly rigorous inspection system. Vehicles must have windshields, of course — and brakes and headlights, the standard items — but I managed to drive my truck for years with a steering malfunction that only I knew about, capable of shaking the wheel from a driver's hands. When I discussed this tic with a neighbor, he advised driving with a pair of Vise-grips handy — right on the dashboard in front of me — to clamp on the nut at the end of the steering column the day the wheel came off. As had happened to him twenty years ago. That way, when the moment of truth came, I would still have a tiller to steer with.

A missing door, however, I felt sure would be noticed by the state's inspection system. So I got the thing remounted and tied it shut with baling twine just like its partner; eventually, I wired one door to the other under the seat of the cab. Then I could drive again — drive legally, I would wager — but entrance to or egress from the truck had to be accomplished through a window.

This got boring fast, so I reluctantly started truck-shopping. April is not a great time for such ventures; the factory year is smack in midseason, the coming warm months are apt to boost sales, and dealers tend to have inventory pretty well balanced with demand. Worse, the sort of guy who buys a truck in April really needs one. I could not disguise my need. Salesmen, peering from their glassy showrooms, could perceive that they had a serious shopper on their hands the instant they saw me squirming out a window of my truck and dropping to the pavement. I might draw myself erect and dust my pants and look discerning, but they knew they had a fish on the line.

"Boy, you need a truck!" they would tell me.

"Well, I'm just out pricing things."

Prices were astonishing. The equivalent of the pickup I had bought in 1972 for three thousand dollars now cost more like *ten*. "Why?" I asked, incredulous.

"We've improved these quite a bit. Corrosion protection, for example. Better mileage. Safety features."

"What's my old truck worth in trade?"

This question tended to bring silence, then a painful wince. But one quite candid salesman pointed to a new spare tire and said: "Your junker's just about worth one of those."

So I quickly ruled out buying new — ten thousand dollars! The truck to buy, I figured, would be three or four years old. Someone else could eat the hefty, early-year depreciation; I would get a moderately priced machine with most of its functional life ahead of it.

Every dealer had a couple of pickup trucks like that on hand, and the remarkable thing was, they had all belonged to relatives or close personal friends of the salesmen who showed them to me. "Nothing wrong with that truck," they would say. "It was my sister's husband's."

"Really?"

"You can see . . . see where the seat's just a little torn there? Biff's a big, big man."

Or again, across town: "That truck, there? That's what you would call a . . . well, special situation. My old hunting partner owns it, and I said I'd try to sell it for him. No commission . . . just one buddy trying to help another, see? And listen: I *know* that truck!"

I saw perhaps a dozen used trucks — all miraculously having belonged to someone's sister, or best friend — and then I narrowed the list down to a few that I would go back and drive. The first of these tests was on a low-mileage, high-sprung, undeniably sharp machine; I climbed behind the wheel ready for adventure. But it wouldn't start — not for me and not for the salesman, either. Battery was dead. "Sit right here," the salesman said. "I'll have a mechanic jump you."

I sat for a while, then had a look under the hood. The battery was dead because the generator wouldn't turn because the fan belt was frayed and loose. When the mechanic roared up, I pointed these things out.

"Sumbitch," he muttered, and tightened the fan belt and started the engine.

"Gas looks mighty low," I mentioned.

"Low? You got a couple of gallons."

Perhaps I did — perhaps that truck was a *champion* guzzler — but halfway across the parking lot the engine coughed and died. Empty. The salesman barked at someone to fetch a can of gasoline, and the mechanic was summoned again to jump-start the truck. By now, though, I was losing interest; amid all the excitement, I managed to slip away.

At another lot, I climbed into a four-wheel-drive, three-quarter-ton hulk. Not knowing how to shift the thing — how to work the transmission transfer case — I asked the salesman for instruction. "Just put it where you want to be," he said.

But there was 2H, 4H, 2L, 4L — confused, I asked, *"Where* do I want to be?"

"2H," he said. "High range. Here, watch . . . " He pushed the shifter toward 2H, and the drive train commenced a sort of civil war, with vivid sound.

"Doesn't sound too good," I commented. He jerked the transfer shift back to neutral.

He said: "Now, there's nothing wrong with this truck. *That* I *know.* For *sure.* Let me go find somebody who knows how to shift the thing."

He went off to find somebody, and I sat behind the wheel. After several minutes an old, toothless geezer wandered over. "They send you to show me how to shift this?"

"Huh?"

"You work here?"

"Hell, no. I'm shopping. Trading trucks. You going to buy this?"

"Maybe. But it doesn't shift right. Problem with the transfer case."

"Huh? Shoot, just 2H? That's *H,* for *Highway.* That's for when you're going down the road. And that *L?* That's *Logging.* That's for when you're logging in the woods. My old truck's just like this. But the transmission's beat. I'm trading."

I was not surprised to hear his truck had shifting problems, too. "Logging in the woods?" I asked.

"Ayup. Been a pretty good year. What's he asking for this truck?"

"Six thousand."

"Holy — why, that bassard! You know what he said he'd give for mine? The same truck? Twenny-two hunnert!"

At that point, I eased out from behind the wheel and sloped off. The restless, troubled truck shopper looking for a sign. I found it at the next stop, where a pickup had been traded in at the ripe age of eight months. Something must certainly have been wrong with it, I figured; but it was still under factory warranty, and the value of having such a contractual guarantee had come to loom large for me. The price, while more than I had hoped, was very considerably less than that of a comparable truck bought new. So I closed a deal, in which my old pickup was credited at about the price of a spare tire. And I drove off in a nearly brand new truck, purchased right.

The transmission popped out of gear three times, just getting home. And over the course of my first two months of ownership, that truck languished in the dealer's shop for nearly six weeks. Its transmission was dropped and rebuilt — *twice* — before it learned to stay in gear. And then, after much vexation, I found myself owning a sturdy, reliable, late-model pickup truck. Just like any prosperous farmer with a good year on his hands.

For any man who thinks his truck is worn out, however, there is someone who will say it's not. Not long after this, I was tooling around town when I saw, with some incredulity, my old pickup lurching across a distant intersection. Oh, it had a new door on it and a few cosmetic touch-ups, but it was my truck. It was someone else's *new* truck — sold, no doubt, as having belonged to someone's wife's brother. Cream puff. Nothing really wrong. And the price? Most likely, more than a spare tire.

I drive with increasing caution, overweening caution, nowadays. When I see an older pickup careening down the highway, trailing blue smoke and brown rust, I know just how slender is the driver's measure of control. He may be a die-hard Yankee, deeply committed to using something till it breaks; but he may be a damned fool, too. And now and then, behind the wheel, I get a little shiver of stark terror. I think: my old junker is still out there, somewhere, still rolling down the road.

CHAPTER FOUR

Sweat Equity

VERMONTERS SEEM PERPETUALLY long on time but short on funds; life here has a way of winnowing out those who cannot tolerate skimpy wages, endless winter nights, and wild fuel bills. But a population that can thrive on such harsh conditions becomes adept at scaling down the cost of living to the point where ends can meet. Thus, Vermonters tend to be their own mechanics and plumbers and electricians — for better or worse. They are their own lumberjacks and greengrocers and butchers, too. But nowhere is the fabled Yankee self-reliance more evident than in the Vermont approach to the challenge of shelter.

In my neck of the woods, it is safe to assume that every citizen of voting age possesses basic carpentry skills. Men and women alike. Half the men, perhaps, have worked for pay in building trades at some point in their lives. Everyone owns his own tools — you can't find a household, for example, that doesn't have its own rafter square. And somebody who understands what all the numbers on it mean.

When I moved to a farm in Vermont a dozen years ago, construction fantasies were uppermost in my mind. There was an old barn to fix up for a place to live; there were sheep barns and machinery sheds and outbuildings to erect; and I dreamed of ultimately building a huge solar house on a grassy knoll with clear southern exposure. But neither my wife nor I, at that point, could aim a hammer at a nail and expect to hit it with any consistency. Higher education had taught us certain skills, like getting high and talking about logical positivism, but nothing very practical. I had never been given cause to examine a rafter square in my life.

I do not begrudge my study of the liberal arts, however. My experience with practical skills convinces me that they can be learned at any age, so long as one is unafraid to look a little foolish. As for slogging through the syllabus of Western civilization, on the other hand, society is wise to launch young people on this journey before they have attained a mature perspective on their lives. Otherwise the academies would empty overnight. One hears all the time about dissatisfied toilers in intellectual vineyards who discover happiness as, say, plumbers; one seldom hears of individuals who go the other way.

At any rate, by the time my wife and I had converted the old barn into a domicile, we had progressed from sheer incompetence to the level of reasonably skilled but somewhat casual carpenters. Confident amateurs, impressed with the perception that buildings almost never collapse. No matter what. Then financial adversity forced on me the good fortune of spending several months working for two highly skilled, dropout-intellectual carpenters, of which Vermont has hundreds. These fellows taught me, with some effort, to saw framing members to rather closer tolerances than the half-inch or so that I thought was reasonable. And they forced me to consider how buildings work: how an array of live and dead loads is efficiently transferred through vertical and horizontal planes down to a foundation engineered to match the structure and the soil conditions.

Armed with increasing skill and knowledge, I got into the habit of taking on a farm construction project every year. Design and execution. Pretty soon, the creation of nifty architectural spaces became no big deal. And when stretched for cash, I could choose trees in my own woodlot to saw up for lumber. When a person owns a pile of lumber on the stump, he does not have to wince nearly so hard at construction costs.

In short, in terms of building skills I have managed to become worthy of my neighbors here. It is a source of endless joy to me. I now *have* the solar house on the grassy knoll — almost — and I fear it's almost time to put away my rafter square; the farm is *over*built, and repair jobs alone are going to plague me for the foreseeable future. New siding on one building, new roof on another — such lists have a way of growing.

Still, it saddens me to think I'm finished with my building phase. The creativity involved is every bit as pure, as hard, and as exciting as that involved in, say, writing. I *know* this. The mechanical aspects of the work — grinding it out, making things fit together — are substantially more interesting and healthful when the work is a building rather than a book. And the clincher is that a book, when finished, is something that its author begins to move away from. In a year, it will embarrass him. In two years, he will never pick it up. In three years, he will recommend to *others* not to pick it up.

A house, though — when one has designed it and refined it and whacked the nails into the boards — a house is a creation one can *live* in, once it's finished. And usually *must* live in, resources being scarce. Thus, the sweat-equity approach to shelter does more than make housing affordable for those who choose to live up here; it forces those who live up here to learn to live with themselves.

• Handyman Specials

Long before I moved upcountry, I had been made familiar with the sort of bargain housing sometimes referred to as a Handyman Special. I had *lived* in Handyman Specials — in California, Pennsylvania, and Massachusetts — without any particular handiness, without improving them in any way during my tenancy. In each of those places, the term referred to older dwellings in need of more than paint but less than, say, a new roof. This was not so in Vermont. Here, I quickly realized, structures that had only marginally averted collapse — that stood upright thanks more to habit than sound carpentry — could be touted and sold as Handyman Specials.

False advertising? Not necessarily; Vermont society assumes a higher quotient of per capita handiness than most. And such housing could be purchased for a song — in fact, sometimes a chorus or two would be deemed sufficient. Then, by investing countless hours of the surplus time that accompanies Vermont life, the purchaser of such a house could gradually upgrade it to civilized standards. Success at this could make a person rich, after a fashion.

Since much of rural Vermont has only recently recouped the population densities of a century ago, our landscape displays a substantial number of older houses that are in dire neglect. But, remarkably, we also have an inventory of *newer* houses that qualify as Handyman Specials, on account of certain social currents of the 1970s. And we have countless *non*houses, many of which also make the grade: crumbling hay barns, one-room schools, long-abandoned chicken coops. Virtually any swaybacked, knock-kneed, rotting structure is in danger of becoming someone's sweat-equity arena.

Most, of course, opt for an older house rather than some geodesic dome or stable. Traditional residential architecture in these parts has an enduring appeal that decades of woeful decay cannot diminish; narrow clapboards, trim shutters, and austere references to the age of Greek Revival can seduce one into overlooking the most glaring structural deficiencies. I have watched a number of my peers acquire such housing, each believing he was undertaking the correction of essentially cosmetic problems. After all, those buildings *stood* — they could be presumed to have a frame, at any rate, of unimpeachable integrity.

In renovation, though, one thing has a way of leading to another. I recall a long weekend spent helping a friend rebuild two gable dormers on the second floor of his vast, rambling, bargain-basement home. After some initial difficulty taking basic measurements, we discovered that one knee wall holding up the roof had drifted badly out of plumb. Trying to correct this fault, we found that an important beam had cracked and slipped out of its mortise in a corner post. That, in turn, led to a significant heave in the foundation wall — and suddenly my friend was in for far more sweat than he had bargained for. And much less equity: although correcting structural faults in an old house can be damned expensive, the costs incurred are quite difficult to pass along to future buyers. Unlike paint, a slate hearth, or a master bath, money spent on structure is practically invisible. Practically down the tubes.

Besides concealing problems of bankrupting potential, older, heavy-timbered houses often frustrate the handyman's efforts to use modern, modular building materials. Plywood and Sheetrock, fiberglass and Styrofoam, prefinished paneling and precut studs — all are created on the assumption that framing members will be neatly spaced on centers of sixteen inches, flush inside and out. "Look at this!" a neighbor of mine wailed, having exposed the guts of his living-room wall. "Those aren't studs, they're baby trees! And they're *round*, not square. And they're on thirty-four-inch centers over here, twenty-nine-inch over there — *nothing's* going to fit this! And they're hundred-year-old hackmatack! I can't even drive a nail in them!"

I had seen such pioneer framing before. "What you have to do," I said, "is build a whole new stud wall just inside the old one. With two-by-fours. Hang your insulation, screw your sheetrock onto that. Then rewire and replumb everything."

"You mean build a whole new house just inboard from the one I've got!"

"You've got the idea," I said.

"Why did I buy *this* one, then?"

I couldn't answer him. I had not been suckered into fixing up an older house; I had bought a barn instead, placing myself squarely in the brotherhood of those who choose *non*houses to make into their homes. A barn, I presumed, could hide few secrets — every element of framing was on public display. Though my skills at carpentry were frankly amateurish — though my handiwork scarcely looked professional — I still had a warm, secure feeling that I could not jeopardize a massively overbuilt structure that had held up for better than a century.

My barn stood on eight huge, hand-hewn posts; each sat on a hefty foundation stone at a point substantially below the layer of manure that covered the earthen floor. When I cleared this well-rotted excrement away, I was astonished to discover *daylight* under six of those eight posts. No bearing whatsoever. Where they had lain swamped in dung, the wood of those great framing members had the approximate consistency of wet cardboard. A child could have crumbled them away.

Disconcerted to find that my future home had no visible means of support, I climbed up in the rafters to investigate a collar tie, a ten-by-ten collar tie, that seemed to have slipped its mortise in the barn's thirty-six-foot-long plate. What I found was rot. And a skimpy iron rod that some thoughtful farmer had installed many years ago to strap the failing joint together.

For one who had not planned to, I learned a great deal about structural issues in post-and-beam frames before my barn conversion job was finished. Well, not exactly finished. Fact is, I can't think of a single Handyman Special in Vermont that can properly be called finished. Owners give up hope periodically, or pause to gather strength for some future spurt of high ambition. One can eat only so much sawdust with one's daily bread. And, in time, unfinished walls acquire such familiarity that they look almost normal.

Several years ago, Vermont performed an important service to the nation by accepting immigrant Whole Earth devotees in numbers wholly disproportionate to the state's tiny size and population. The newcomers wanted — if one takes them at their word — to Go Back To The Land. Almost unconsciously, they recognized a point of ideology where the existing, conservative Vermont ethos merged with their desire to foster a "greening" of America: both extremes shared a mania for unfettered individualism, for personal liberty. But as ideologues are wont to do, the newcomers sought new architectural forms that would give concrete expression to their deeply held beliefs and values. Almost overnight, unique and organic and sculptural residences began to emerge from a landscape formerly renowned for restrained, homogeneous, white clapboard houses.

In itself, this architectural revolution might not have produced a bumper crop of late-model Handyman Specials, but it was a tenet of the back-to-the-land set that each person ought to design *and build* his natural abode. Whether he knew how to or not. Many of these immigrants had squandered their prime hammer-swinging years in universities, pursuing advanced degrees; they came to construction work with a minimum of practical experience. And a maximum of philosophical baggage.

I remember particularly from that era a generalized abhorrence of the right angle. Right angles were deemed dull and cold and obsessively rational, a symbol of excessive cultural rigidity. Compared with, say, spherical icosahedrons. Geodesics never came to dominate the alternative architecture in these parts, however; weird trapezoidal shapes pierced at unlikely angles by rhomboidal turrets and hexagonal atria better suited the local fancy. Such buildings were very hard indeed for amateurs to frame. They were more difficult to sheathe and make watertight, and utterly defeating when it came to interior finish work. Nobody, no matter what he smoked, could handle all those angles.

After only a few years, such houses had a way of coming onto the market as Handyman Specials. When somebody bought one, he would organize a work party, to engage his friends and neighbors in the challenge of making these odd spaces habitable. No skills were required to attend such a party, and an aspiring builder like myself could learn a lot and make mistakes on someone else's home and castle. So, for several years, I was an avid party-goer.

Typical of that era were the work parties my wife and I attended on behalf of a young woman who had purchased — *third*-hand — one of these not-so-old but wild houses. The second owner had succumbed after fitting and taping Sheetrock to an interesting living-room ceiling that had thirty-seven facets. Having such a carefully finished surface in one room helped visitors imagine how nice the whole house might someday be; but, for a dwelling that had been inhabited for some time, the overall degree of unfinish was amazing.

The work parties began when the new owner revealed a dangerous state of mind after only half a year's residency. On the day she took possession, she had made a nifty list of things that needed doing right away — in the first week, say. It was quite a long list. She had taped it to the door of her kerosene-fueled refrigerator, eager to check off jobs as she completed them; but after a full six months, she had made only one check: "Replace ladder to second floor with staircase." Most unfortunately for her state of mind, this staircase had failed.

The first of her work parties drew more than twenty people. Many had rather keen carpentry skills, and by day's end they had expressed considerable contempt for the owner-builder-architect who had spawned such a boondoggle. Like it or not, one of them pointed out sagely, *plumbness* is at right angles to *levelness*. Every time. Houses that are not framed plumb and level are apt to encounter profound difficulties in the long run. In the short run, placing building planes at right angles to each other makes many aspects of construction a hell of a lot easier than more organic alternatives.

After a day's work it was surprising how little had been accomplished by twenty-odd eager people. The second work party attracted only eight people, and the third drew fewer than that. Then the owner hired a pair of extremely masochistic carpenters, who spent the entire winter taming selected portions of that unruly dwelling. Sweat equity be damned.

To a remarkable extent, those who take on Handyman Specials in Vermont grew up in suburban split-levels in places like New Jersey. The pendulum swings, and cultural excesses are balanced against one another. Where will it all end? I think I know. With each passing year, even I have to confess to a growing attraction to trailers. Mobile homes, that is. Their utter sensibility; their quiet, simple elegance. Their allusion to the possibility of motion. Their stunning absence of equity. Their unabashed absence of sweat. I predict for such housing a very bright future.

• Form and Function

Some postindustrial artists haven't the faintest idea how an engine works, but are competent to weld sculptures out of old pistons, worn crankshafts, broken gears, and other scrap from the nearest auto graveyard. Found art, more or less. These exercises in pure form never bothered me till I moved to Vermont, joining a society in which aesthetic values run a distant second to mechanical know-how. Then I realized that in my practical neighbors' eyes, such uninformed use of hard, cold steel would be ludicrous.

I knew little about mechanics when I moved upcountry, but then I had no desire to weld junk sculptures, either. *Had* I wanted to, though, I would have been in fat city: walking the acreage that my wife and I had rashly purchased, I was surprised to see how many used farm machines had been thrown in with my real-estate deal. Hidden in a maple grove behind the swamp was an ancient corn chopper, an odd place for such a tool. Nestled near the foot of the cliff was a three-bottom plow with two cracked bottoms. Tucked among a stand of cedars was a heavy, complicated instrument for cultivating field corn. And there were a couple of unabashed junk piles, to which my predecessors had evidently been consigning worn-out scraps of metal for decades.

I was mildly curious as to how the more substantial items of machinery came to be stashed around my farm. So I asked a neighbor.

"It was Donaldson," he informed me. "He was going bankrupt, and the bank guys were coming out to repossess whatever they could get their hands on. So he took his machinery and hid it on them — just to spite the bankers, understand? Some of it they found. Some they didn't. Some of it, nobody's ever going to find."

"And now what's there is mine?" I asked.

"Hell, yes. Not worth much now, anyway."

They *weren't* worth much, as farm machines, but it wasn't long before I came to value this scattered collection of hard, cold steel. The barn I was proposing to convert into my house had several disturbing structural features, the worst of which was that its east and west walls were attempting to head *farther* east and west, respectively. Rotten collar tie met rotten plate. Some prudent farmer — Donaldson? — had years ago installed an iron rod to slow this process, but the rod was definitely losing the battle. Besides, it did not fit in with our planned interior. So, taking some neighborly advice, I ventured forth to buy two long lengths of five-eighths-inch steel cable. By looping each around bearing posts on the west and east walls, then cinching them together with a monster turnbuckle, we could draw the barn's sides back together. Then we'd hide the cable in the framing of the upstairs floor, incorporating it into the building forever.

There was just one problem, though, and we heard about it from seven hardware dealers in a row. "Can't sell you a turnbuckle big enough to do that job," they said.

"Why not?"

"Because they don't make them anymore."

Six hardware dealers shrugged, a gesture these fellows must learn in hardware school. The seventh — a sly, balding old Yankee — said, "Used to be a great big turnbuckle built into the Dearborn plow. The old Dearborns. To adjust the bottoms."

"So?"

"If you could find a farmer with that plow out in his junk heap . . ."

I went home and took a walk. And, by golly, *I* had that old plow in my junkheap! It took a can of Liquid Wrench, a propane torch, and lots of patience, but I got that turnbuckle off. Next morning I began to cinch my barn together. It was frightening work. I would take a couple of turns on the turnbuckle, then my wife and I would evacuate the barn for half an hour while it creaked and groaned and redistributed long-accumulated stresses. By evening, though, the old barn's sidewalls were nearly as plumb as on the day they had been raised.

Having achieved this wonderful feat, I could not bring myself to bury the turnbuckle within a partition. I wanted to *expose* it, like . . . well, like sculpture, I suppose. A functional sculpture. So I framed the main entry door directly beneath it; and now every time someone enters the house he can see that turnbuckle and reflect briefly on the usefulness of junk. Of found objects. Of the very stuff of postindustrial objets d'art.

Eventually, we ceased to call our barn a barn and began referring to it as our house. We were house-proud, too. Our hay-loft-size living room was big enough to hold several of the urban apartments we had formerly occupied. It had a cathedral ceiling — naturally — and exposed, hand-hewn beams. This mammoth space, we felt, simply cried out for a work of sculpture — a heavy chandelier, say — to absorb some of its sheer volume.

Our corner of Vermont boasts a substantial population of craftspeople and artisans, all doing their best to prolong the end of the 1960s. Several of them work in metal, and a weaver friend named Janet suggested I approach one welder in particular about a chandelier for our hayloft living room. I had never commissioned a work of art in my life, though, and had no idea how to proceed, or how to assess the value of any such piece. So I tabled my friend's suggestion, and for months our cathedral ceiling remained open and airy.

Then one night we all found ourselves at the same Halloween party — the weaver, the metal sculptor, my wife, and me. Since it is good manners for one hippie artisan to drum up business for another, Janet soon introduced us all. The sculptor was a mountain of a man, and he was drunk. Astonishingly drunk. He struggled to get his eyes focused as I shook his hand. I said, "Yes, I've heard about you. I thought I might ask you about making me a sculpture. A chandelier, actually."

He stared wildly, trying hard to follow. Finally he bellowed, "Huh?"

". . . make a sculpture?"

The metal sculptor took a deep breath, which brought him up to seven feet. Then he went to find a fresh beer. Then he came back, slurped it, and said: "Whuzzu want, a lot of old pistons and crap all dangling down? With light bulbs sticking out?"

"Well, I thought I'd let you see the space and hear what you suggest."

"Huh? What I suggest? Huh?"

"That was my idea."

"You got a lot of bucks?"

"Not a lot, but I thought maybe . . . "

"Here's what I suggest: make your own damn chandelier. Huh?"

"Uh-huh," I nodded. Janet looked at me and shrugged, just like a hardware dealer. And that was that, as far as my commissioning a work of art was concerned.

Next day, I tramped my woods from one concealed hunk of farm machinery to the next. I sensed artistic opportunities in worn roller chains, dull chopper knives, and pitted plow colters; but after much contemplation I settled on a wheel rim from the old corn cultivator. It was badly damaged — out of round, missing several spokes, terminally corroded — but it was big and hefty and possessed a certain agrarian *je ne sais quoi*. I rolled it home and reamed out half a dozen of the spoke holes around its circumference; into these holes I fitted oversize Christmas-tree lights. They weren't the kind that are supposed to blink, but for reasons I don't fully understand, they *did* blink. Utterly at random. An intermittent thermal connection, I suppose, involving all that surrounding steel.

"I don't know," my wife said when I showed her my work of art.

"Look, it didn't cost a cent."

"Wouldn't have fooled me, either."

"Man who builds his own house has a right to decorate it, too."

"How are you going to hang that thing?" she wondered. "It looks awfully heavy."

"I thought I might try an iron rod."

"Delicate touch," she sniffed.

But I *had* an iron rod, the very same one that had spent years strapping the barn together before I replaced it with the cable-

and-turnbuckle. What more fitting way to retire it, I thought, than to make it the suspension system for my blinking chandelier.

No one, not in ten years, has ever asked me whom I commissioned to produce the postindustrial sculpture hanging from that hayloft ceiling. Nor has anybody asked how much a person has to spend to obtain such a creation. Sometimes people wonder, though, what the hell kind of wheel that is. Then I answer, knowledgeably: "Think it's from an old-fashioned corn cultivator."

"Really?" the questioner will nod, overwhelmed by wisdom.

"And you know what?" I will press on. "I haven't the faintest idea how it works."

To belt one's house together with a piece of industrial scrap — of found art — brings a certain satisfaction; but to hang such a piece from the ceiling — an exercise in pure, mindless form — is to have one's credentials as an artist made secure. It's nice to know I have enough junk on my hands to cover any need.

• Trial Balloon

One of my oldest ambitions — going back, at least, to a science fair in seventh grade — has been to build a solar house of my own design. A better-organized person might have pursued such a goal straightforwardly: by enrolling, say, in an architectural school, or by becoming a builder. I have let my life wander on devious paths, however — paths with no apparent relation to solar construction. I have shuffled aimlessly. Nevertheless, two years ago I broke ground on the domicile of my dreams, and I have every hope of occupying the result sometime in the near future. Rome, after all, wasn't built in a day.

My vague conceptions for a house got a big lift several years ago when I signed up for a tour of selected solar houses in the rural county where I live. This is a measure of how hot the new architecture has become in this chilly, windswept valley; nearly everybody has a solar dream house in mind or bold plans to retrofit present accommodations with a greenhouse full of heat-collecting gear. A day spent visiting existing installations and discussing their pros and cons with the folks who knew them best seemed a very sensible way to refine one's visions.

Fifty-four souls, a busful, subscribed to this novel tour, and all expressed surprise when the aforementioned bus turned out to be a *school* bus, and an ancient one at that. Just about ready to be turned over to hippies. After boarding this conveyance, on a bright but cold November morn, two phenomena became quickly evident. First, an old bus used to hauling sixty-pound school-children had its work cut out to haul one-hundred-sixty-pound adults. Second, solar houses are apt to be erected rather far off the beaten track. On remote hilltops, say. At the end of long, steep, rock-strewn driveways. The site was the thing; and after all, no oil trucks or meter readers need call.

Then a third and disconcerting truth emerged from our visits: the owners of solar houses cannot objectively discuss the merits and demerits of such dwellings. These folks are firm partisans. They have voted, awesomely, with their wallets. Conversing with such devotees, one never hears of solar failures. A system's pay-back potential — the time required to recoup its cost in fuel sav-ings — might be slight indeed; still, its owners could be relied upon to tout it as a huge success.

Our school bus sloughed off several minor portions of itself — exhaust components, mirrors, reflectors — in the tricky drive-ways to the first two houses on our tour. Then, while cruising a stretch of paved road across the county, a front tire exploded. Like a cannon firing. The wheel rim broke in two, and, with heroic effort, the young driver brought the bus to rest near a roadside ditch. We fans of solar heat tumbled out, feeling dazed but lucky. Getting a second bus to come rescue the tour took a couple of hours, however, during which time the tourists could do little more than shuffle about in the cold.

During this unexpected hiatus, I cornered a solar-design ex-pert and tried to pick his brains about a trial balloon I had in mind, a passive solar atrium added to the south end of my barn/house. Something simple. Something on the cheap.

The word offended him: "You mean inexpensive?"

"I mean cheap."

"*How* cheap?"

"Well, I've only got five thousand dollars tied up in my whole house. I think ten percent of that would . . . "

"Solar? For five hundred bucks?"

"Cheap," I nodded. "Just a little hundred-square-foot addi-tion. Five dollars per foot — hey, that's *twice* what I've been building for."

He sniffed. "New solar construction costs start at *fifty* dollars per square foot. And the sky's the limit."

"I'll just have to be resourceful, then."

"And passive," he said. "Very, very passive. Glass wall, concrete floor. Period. Keep it simple. Don't get carried away with fancy stuff like you'll see today."

A large tow truck arrived, just then, to carry away our school bus, and eventually a second bus arrived to transport us to the balance of the solar houses on the tour. We were shown black canisters of phase-change eutectic salts, photovoltaic arrays, and elaborate panels that used sunlight to heat air or water or antifreeze solutions for circulation throughout the house. We saw out-of-state megabucks gone solar, but I kept repeating: Passive. Glass and concrete. Cheap.

I knew I could pour concrete cheaply, since I own a little mixer and have stayed on good terms with the local gravel magnate. Cheap glass was a tough one, though. Consulting with a carpenter friend, I was advised to check replacement panes for sliding glass doors. A shrewd suggestion. Even these, though, proved to exceed my modest budget. What I had to find was glass that had, metaphorically, fallen off a truck. Glass like that is hard to come by.

I spent a good half year on the lookout for cheap glass, and then lightning struck. It struck in the form of a skyscraper project in Montreal rejecting an acre or so of glass — tempered, safety, insulated skyscraper glass in sheets that measured six feet high by thirty inches wide. The problem was a moderate distortion in the product: if you stood in front of one of those plates and did a deep knee bend, the landscape would gently ripple before your eyes. Imperfect; but such glass, I figured, would be certain to reduce substantially its owner's liquor bill. The glass was being dumped in southern Quebec at giveaway prices — prices just too good to resist.

There is in Vermont a Natural Organic Farmer's Association comprising highly ideological and under-capitalized tillers of the soil. This organization used to pool its members' orders to obtain great quantities of fish meal, leather meal, and similar organic plant foods; located in Quebec, the supplier of these offbeat fertilizers had gotten its hands on several crates of skyscraper glass. Card-carrying Natural Organic Farmers could obtain the stuff for thirty-eight dollars the pane.

I had never joined the Natural Organic Farmers, and had drifted a good distance from their persuasion over several years of shepherding; but I now applied for membership and was not disappointed. Three panes of the Montreal glass would have satisfied my needs for the solar atrium. The more I thought about it, though, the more I became convinced I'd never see insulated glass at such a price again. If I ever really were going to build a solar house, now was the time to stretch for it.

I bought a crate: twenty-five panes of glass. This obliterated, of course, my proposed budget for the trial balloon. But it made my commitment to an eventual solar house feel strong indeed; and the expense of glazing, I well knew, was the chief derailer of ambitious solar plans. I stored the glass carefully in the machinery shed, took a deep breath, and started tearing off the south wall of my dwelling.

In doing so, I discovered something most alarming. I had always maintained a laissez-faire attitude toward such bothersome and tedious problems as mice; the knowledge that I had a few vermin living in the walls that protected me from the elements did not disturb my sleep. But it was amazing to behold the damage they had done in a mere seven or eight years of residence: fiberglass batting had been mined to form substantial nests, wiring had been chewed bare of its plastic insulation, and endless dark passages assured an easy flow of air from the outside to the inside of my house. And vice versa. No wonder I had found myself burning more and more wood with each passing winter.

Now, solar heat presumes extremely high standards of overall construction, in order to minimize infiltration of cold air into a building. There is little to be gained by going solar in a house that manifestly leaks like a sieve. And as my south wall went, so went those to the north, east, and west: innocent rodents had imperiled the thermal integrity of my dwelling.

I bit the bullet. I stripped each wall of its old exterior siding, reinsulated and rewired and resheathed each in rodent-resistant fashion. Then I got a cat, and mousetraps. By the time I got back to the south wall where I had begun, several months had passed and I was a great deal poorer.

Winter, though, was closing in. I had a solar room to build before snow began flying, or else I had a catastrophe on my hands.

Passive solar architecture is not hard to understand; one arranges things so that sunlight penetrates a building and strikes an appropriate thermal storage mass. The mass may be a liquid, such as water; it may be an interior masonry wall; but in the case of my trial balloon it was to be an eight-inch-thick concrete slab painstakingly insulated from the earth beneath it. This slab, just inboard from my new south wall of three skyscraper glass panes, would store up solar heat on sunny days and radiate it back into my house all night. While contributing only very modestly to my house's heat requirements, the slab would nonetheless act as a huge thermal flywheel, moderating extreme swings in internal temperature. And it would offer us a place for winter sunbathing.

I did a creditable job of building this addition; by Thanksgiving, I could make claim to living in a partially solar house. Or solar barn, an even more distinctive feat. I was not pleased, however, with the aesthetics of a bare concrete floor in this atrium, which opened onto several downstairs rooms. It cried out to be covered. So I sought the advice of the solar engineer who had shared his expertise with me the year before, on the memorable house tour. "What can I put on that concrete," I asked, "that won't impair its function?"

"Slate," he answered. "Dark slate. I thought you were too cheap for frills, though."

"That plain slab is mighty ugly."

"Spend your five hundred dollars, yet?"

I reviewed for him, then — with complete candor — the unfortunate history of my little project. By the time I had rebuilt all four outer walls of my house, I figured I had paid for the place all over again. At least it would finally be tight as a drum. So that solar heat might have a chance.

My misfortunes left him unfazed. He said, "Another couple hundred bucks for slate won't kill you, then. Or a couple hundred more to hire a good mason."

But I was far too shrewd to shell out that kind of money. Rather than have a supplier truck slate out to me at some exorbitant price, I drove my junker pickup truck half a day south to a quarry, where I dickered with two brothers in the slate business. Reject slates, I wanted. Seconds. They had piles and piles of them. I negotiated a most favorable price, and drove away smiling. For about two and a half miles, during which time my pickup steered with the agility of a supertanker. Slate is heavy; I had grossly underestimated just *how* heavy. Some critical element in my rear suspension broke, and then a tire blew to smithereens. Déjà vu. Several days and several trips later, I had my slate. *And* my truck, only marginally worse for wear. But when I priced slate retail, I found I had driven no bargain.

That was not the worst, though. Certainly I had no need to hire a good mason at ten or fifteen bucks an hour to lay flat, square slates on a concrete floor; it wasn't as though the project might fall over, like a chimney. So I laid the slates atop my slab in a thick, gooey bed of tile mastic, and the result looked worthy of *House Beautiful*. Overnight, however, the sunroom's thermal properties changed. For the worse: the dark slate surface grew uncomfortably warm in afternoon sunlight — almost too hot to walk on — and then it cooled to toe-numbing temperatures shortly after nightfall.

I called the expert. "Why?"

"You mean you didn't set those slates down in *mortar?*"

"Gee, no, I . . . "

"That tile mastic isn't dense enough. It's almost like a layer of air. What happens is, it insulates your slates *away from* the concrete slab. So all that underlying mass is bound to go to waste — no thermal storage, see? No flywheel."

"Shoot," I said — or something like that. "Well, it was only an experiment. A trial balloon, for something bigger. Nothing to do but learn from my mistakes."

"You hire the right architect," the wise man suggested, "and you won't have to *make* mistakes. Or at least . . ." — and here he chuckled — "at least you'll make more *interesting* mistakes."

"Sorry," I said. "Not my style. And I can't afford it, either."

So the solar atrium was essentially a failure. No one has to know that, though. People see the glass façade on an old hay barn's south wall, and they're likely to think: there's somebody else who's entered the solar age. And when anybody asks me how the place is working out, I put on the confident smile of the solar owners I met on that bus tour. "Yessir," I tell them. "Free heat. Worth every penny of it."

• Architectural Services

After the trial balloon, I still had twenty-two sheets of sky-scraper glass tucked away in the machinery shed, and having it there made the solar-house design process vastly easier than it had been before. Before, my house had been a series of vague ideas and tentative shapes; every winter I had made a few more cardboard models, none of them quite satisfying. Now, though, I knew something mighty important about it. I knew that its south façade was going to have twenty-two big sheets of glass on it, and *that* meant the south façade had room for very little else. What's more, using all that glass in a residence of sane proportions almost dictated that the house should be two stories high.

Sketching this severe and geometric façade, I realized my house could make explicit reference to the traditional New England garrison saltbox. A study of the region's architectural history convinced me that this shape was a consciously passive-solar design, within the limitations of colonial building materials. A garrison saltbox was oriented to the south, and the short cantilever of its second story over the first would shade much of the glazing from the sun at midsummer angles, without impeding winter gains. The north wall, the cold one, was foreshortened to reduce its area and seldom pierced by windows; most of the roof was pitched to the north, where snow could accumulate and help to insulate the building.

I proposed to forge a cunning union of the old and the new, wedding the garrison saltbox form to my crate of skyscraper glass. Inside the house, I planned a two-story atrium centered on the south façade — a soaring sunroom — around which the living spaces on both floors would be arranged in horseshoe fashion. By means of interior windows and sliding glass doors, each room could be opened to the atrium's light and warmth when it was producing heat; but when skies were cold and cloudy — when there was no solar gain — I could close off the heated portions of the house from the vast sunspace, using it only as a buffer between warmth and winter.

Extremely smug about this grand conception, I made a last cardboard model and hired a backhoe to excavate the site. Almost immediately the hoe scraped its teeth on ledge; hard, smooth, monolithic ledge just a foot or two beneath the tired sod. Talk about thin soils! I had the operator crawl a few feet westward and try again — same thing. Then to the north. After tearing up a lot of turf, we found a place where the house could be built with a cellar of highly variable but adequate height. The only problem was, there was no way to get water to drain out of this future basement; just a passing thunderstorm on the evening after the dig turned the hole into a lake, which I then had to siphon dry.

Stumped, I did something that I had sworn I would never stoop to, something wholly out of keeping with my dedication to a vernacular architecture. I called up an architect. Vermont has not so many architects as intellectual-dropout carpenters, but we have a surprising number of them nonetheless. Many are quite talented, with practical construction experience as well as book-learning. But I wanted badly to be the *auteur* of my solar house, and not to have my clear-headed, personal creation diluted by an expert's suggestions, however wise. Still, I also wanted to make that site work without a basement full of water. So I phoned a man who lives up my road and asked him to come have a look.

"Blast," he said.

"But . . . where? How?"

"That'll be up to your blaster. They have ways to fissure ledge so water can drain out of it. Good blaster ought to do that without messing up your hole. This rock will be great stuff to pin a foundation to."

"Pin?"

"You're going to *have* to pin the foundation to the ledge. No other way. Drill and set steel rods every few feet, all around the perimeter. Otherwise, your whole house is apt to slide someday."

I was beginning to get the profound attack of vertigo that I feared a professional might inspire in me. But when the man asked just what sort of house I had in mind, I took him to examine my latest cardboard model. He was, in a way, impressed. "This'll keep you out of trouble for a little while," he said.

"Thing of it is," I bragged, "I just happen to be sitting on all that glass."

He studied the arrangement of my two-story atrium. "You know how you're going to frame this?" he asked politely.

"Well, I . . . I have a few ideas."

"I don't think the south wall of that cantilevered second story ought to bear the roof. Not to mention the *snow* load. I mean, I don't see how it *can*. With that big two-story space, you've got no floor joists tying the load on that cantilever back into the house."

I scratched my head, thinking: buildings never collapse — or *almost* never. I said: "Guess I'll have to think of something."

"I'd design that one framing detail with great care. If I were you."

I said, "Maybe I could run my solution past you, when I figure it out."

"Maybe."

"You know," I said, a trifle lamely, "I don't want to have any conventional architect-client relationship. *I* want to do this. But since you're right there up the road, I would like to be able to pick your brains from time to time. And when you think I owe you some money, I want you to bill me. Fair?"

"I was thinking you could pay me back in other ways," he answered coolly.

"I could?"

"For example, I'm going away next week. To a conference. I'm going to need someone to take care of my boys."

Now, I did not know that the architect had boys. I thought his kids were grown-ups. But if in fact he did have children, why, then a week's baby-sitting seemed an outrageous compensation to suggest for a bit of off-the-cuff architectural advice. I said, "You need a sitter?"

"No," he laughed. "My boys are oxen. Red Man and White Man. I just need them fed and walked out to pasture."

"Sign me up," I told him happily. And I agreed to drop by in a couple of days to learn his chores.

Meanwhile, I called one of the blasters he had mentioned to me. A young, stocky, vigorous man came to see the site, and he knew within ten minutes what he planned to do. I could see the man liked dynamite, *loved* dynamite, and he was full of vivid stories attesting to its power and his skill. The stories were set in Vietnam, at mountain condo sites, and along various highway right-of-ways, but they all had the same exciting climax: *Ka-boom!*

The blaster said my fissure was a mere day's work — four hundred dollars, nearly half of it for dynamite. We set a tentative date and shook hands; he departed.

Now, it happened that my first day with Red Man and White Man was also the day of the big boom. My morning chore was to walk the oxen from their barn stalls to a pasture, where I would tether them to judiciously chosen trees. Each ox was attached to a fifty-foot chain massive enough to enable it to skid logs from my forest; but with or without such leads, one does not walk an ox anywhere that the ox doesn't want to go. Eventually I got the boys staked out to sturdy trees proximate enough for bovine congeniality, but not so proximate that they could tie themselves up in some dangerous and incredible knot. I left them grazing hungrily, and considered what an odd way this was to hire an architect.

Back at my place, the master blaster was busily boring holes into my ledge. He drilled two lines of holes, about a foot apart, from the lowest sump of the cellar hole to a place where his instinct for geology convinced him that the ledge must crest and drop off into very deep clay. Whenever he turned off his exceedingly noisy drill, he would regale me with another remembrance of blasts past; late in the afternoon, he stuffed a stick of dynamite into each of fifty holes and wired one line of holes to detonate a split second before the other. This differential shock wave, he assured me, would fissure the rock and create what amounted to a gutter and floor drain in my future basement.

He led me uphill in my pasture just a little ways — no hard hats, no bunkers — and we squatted down on the grass for the blowout. The dynamite kid's eyes glowed with intense excitement — oh, he loved his work. "Fire in the hole!" he shouted, in accord with some etiquette of his trade. Then he hit the plunger. Rocks, including several rocks at least as big as basketballs, shot out of the hole, along with a tremendous amount of smoke and dust. The ground positively shook; a neighbor's house shook violently several hundred yards away. Under a low ceiling of dense, gray clouds, the shock wave of the blast was reflected back to earth to disturb neighbors and animals for several miles around.

I thought the fun was over when my free-lance blaster stood abruptly, looked skyward, and started walking farther uphill — carefully. This was maybe eight seconds after the detonation. Looking up, I saw a little shower of slivered rock start to sprinkle down on us. Back from the stratosphere. "Just . . . be . . . cool . . ." the man said softly. "Just . . . look . . . up . . . step . . . aside . . ." Miraculously, neither of us took any direct hits. Then we went to look in the foundation hole.

There was not a drop of water left.

I paid the man his wages and excused myself to go perform my ox chores. When I got to the architect's pasture, though, his boys were not in sight. They had *broken their chains*, and, somehow, I knew the exact second when it had happened. Two miles away: *Ka-boom!*

Half an hour later, I sighted Red Man and White Man cowering in a scruffy woodlot; by teasing the galumphing pair with a pail of grain, I eventually got them back to their barn stalls. The architect never knew. Sometimes, though, I think: what if I had lost my charges? What if they had hoofed it into the next county, never to be seen again? Then I think: I would do what any house-proud homeowner does when things don't turn out exactly right. I would blame my architect.

• A Calculated Q

My site excavation and associated blast were accomplished as the winter of 1983–84 closed in. I had no hope of starting to pound nails till the next summer, but knowing precisely how the house would fit into its hole helped me finish the design process during the cold months. I had time on my hands — who doesn't, in February? — and I got the notion to confront the architect's objections to my cardboard model by building a completely thorough framing model of the house. In the scale of one to eight, bigger than the typical dollhouse scale, even.

This project kept me occupied for several weeks. Every stud and joist and rafter was precisely represented; every joint was quite accurately depicted. I used up a quart of casein glue and several tins of brads, and the finished model was actually strong enough for my kids to climb on — for a while, anyhow. As for the problem of the dangling cantilever, I solved it quite niftily by building the roof using trusses rather than mere rafters. The trusses were modified to be supported on their bottom chord over the plane of the foundation wall; a thick beam supported them inboard of the cantilever, bearing the roof load across the two-story atrium. As for the cantilevered wall, it then only had to bear its own weight, no complicated feat.

Building the big model not only helped me pass the winter and solve framing problems; it enabled me to estimate materials with deadly accuracy, and to convey my vision of the house quite efficiently to the pair of dropout-intellectual carpenters that I planned to hire to build it with me. And it gave me something that a solar design consultant could sink his teeth into, calculating the Q of my proposed house.

A building's Q, the product of several pages of algebraic scribbling, is its estimated heat loss per hour per degree Fahrenheit of difference between the thermostat setting inside the house and the ambient temperature outside the house. This heat loss is expressed in British thermal units, or Btus. A properly calculated Q is no small deal; it should give appropriate weight to the thermal properties of all the various building shell components. Once arrived at, it is the key to sizing solar storage mass or any other heating and cooling systems.

I had no confidence that I could calculate a Q correctly, so I engaged a solar design consultant to take on this project for me. Solar design consultants — in these parts, anyway — tend to be dropout-intellectual carpenters moonlighting with their calculators and hoping for better things; the expert I turned up smelled of incense, wore a pony tail, and drove a psychedelic version of my own junker pickup. He would as happily have built my house as crunched some numbers on it, and I have no doubt as to his competence for either task. I loaned him my house model, which he packed into his pickup truck, and for the sort of hourly fee one pays a carpenter he evaluated its thermal properties.

When he was finished, we arranged a meeting. He announced the building's Q, the magic number, would be 325 Btus per hour per degree of temperature differential.

"That's good . . . right?" I asked.

"It's good," he shrugged. "Not great. Just good. I put your Design Heat Load at 23,000 Btus per hour."

"That's a lot of heat," I said. "What does Design Heat Load mean?"

"It means the amount of heat you'll need to keep the house at sixty-five degrees when it's twelve below zero outside. Sort of a worst-case heating scenario. Any average furnace can put out a lot more heat than that."

"Furnace? But this is a *solar* house."

"Only to a certain degree," he said. "I calculated your Solar Fraction at twenty-seven percent."

"That's all?" I was dumbfounded. Crestfallen, too. "Twenty-two plates of glass staring at the winter sun, and I can't even get a third of my heat from it?"

"Sorry," he said. "First, this is a big house. Maybe too big for the glazed area. Second, you haven't designed enough mass into it. Slates on a concrete slab — it's fine, but it's not enough. You can't store enough of the solar heat you'll get, as is. Third — now, this gets tricky — the assumptions behind Solar Fraction calculations are awfully conservative. Deliberately so."

"I'll bet," I said. "Like what?"

"Like, it's assumed that any time the sun heats your house to more than sixty-five degrees — which it often will — it's assumed you spill that extra heat. By venting it outdoors."

"Well, Jeezum! Why would I do that?"

"It's just the way we figure things. In practice, though, most people with a house like this allow the heat to build right up. Seventy, seventy-five — and then the mass gets overcharged, to carry the house better after dark. In practice, solar houses tend to outperform their calculations. Sometimes by a lot."

"I still need a central heating system, though — that's your verdict?"

"Look, it's no big deal. Get a wood furnace for your basement. Forced hot air. In wood, I could see you burning maybe two cords per winter."

"Two cords?" I smiled now. "My old barn-house can burn *eight*. I can cut two cords of wood in one long day's work."

"There's a lot of used wood furnaces around now, too," the design expert told me. "People bought them out of hysteria when the energy crunch hit. Now, though, they're back to oil."

"If you were me," I asked, "and you could change one thing about this house, what would it be?"

He didn't have to think for long. He said: "I would double your storage mass. I would put it on a vertical collecting surface, like the back wall of your sunroom, as well as on a floor slab. In a house like this, it isn't easy to have too much mass."

"Thanks a lot," I said. And paid him.

Just as he had said, the classified ads were full of used wood furnaces. And most of them were behemoths capable of spewing out 100,000 Btus per hour, or enough to heat my house, I figured, at 228 degrees below zero. Heat like that I didn't need. But I liked the concept of a furnace in the basement; wood heat is dirty heat, on account of dust and soot, bark and ashes, and the inevitable snow or mud tracked in with a load of firewood. Keeping all that mess down in the cellar had profound appeal.

Then I started seeing ads for *add-on* furnaces. Checking these out, I realized that they were just what my consultant had had in mind. Mainly produced in the early 1970s, an add-on furnace was designed to sit right next to an oil furnace and borrow its ductwork when the owner built a wood fire. Not a big fire, and not a big firebox, either. When the wood was all burned up, the oil burner would kick back on.

For many reasons, these wood add-on furnaces seldom lived up to their owner's expectations. A chief explanation was that wood fires provide continuous and low-grade heat, whereas oil burners provide periodic bursts of quite intense heat; consequently, central hot-air ducts designed for oil installations often were too small to carry wood heat effectively. Another explanation, no doubt just as rational, is that people with oil furnaces got bored fast with running down cellar to refuel a fire. It was easier to become accustomed to a hefty fuel bill.

Typical of this wood-heat demise was the residence, a stone's throw from a huge I.B.M. factory, where I picked up a wood furnace for my new house at a tiny fraction of its original price. The furnace was in the basement of a flashy tract house in a suburban subdivision the likes of which did not exist anywhere in Vermont fifteen years ago. The owner explained that he had purchased his house on a wooded, two-acre lot. Within a couple of years he had managed to burn up every stick of firewood on the lot, and since then the add-on furnace had sat languishing. This man wanted *out* of wood heat; he threw in a tubular steel firewood rack, a nice set of fireplace tools, a bellows, and eighteen feet of stainless stovepipe to sweeten the already sweet deal on his furnace. And I drove off a happy man.

In the spring — before the ground had thawed, though — I moved the furnace into the cellar hole and set it on the bare ledge. Things like furnaces are easier to put into a house before the house is there, I reckoned. By now, I was spending maybe half an hour a day just poking around the excavated hole, thinking. Meditating. *How* was I going to double the house's storage mass? It wasn't as simple as doubling the thickness of the concrete slab; six inches plus slate was its optimal thickness for putting heat in and taking it out over a twenty-four-hour cycle. I just didn't like the concrete wall my expert had proposed; it meant a whole lot more foundation and a lot more money. There were countless problems integrating it into my framing model. Rolling in the furnace, though —

a chunky, heavy, awkward object — got me musing on what else I might lower in that rock-bottomed hole. *Before* I built a house.

And then, late one night, I sat right up in bed and cried: "Eureka!"

• Club Vermont

Inspiration comes in a variety of forms, and sometimes the use of an old and prosaic product in a new, unheard-of way can be as creative as designing something from thin air. So it was that on that night, up to my ears in final details of the solar house, I woke up my wife to tell her we would have a pool in it. Built right into the floor of its two-story sunroom.

Since it was nearly two in the morning — she had been trying to sleep while I tossed and turned in an architectural fit — she was not inclined to protest. "Good," she said. "But why?"

"Because water is the perfect passive solar-heat storage medium. Pound for pound, water is tremendously efficient. You know what a Btu is?"

She groaned. "What's a Btu?"

"British thermal unit. How we measure heat. When you raise the temperature of one pound of water by one degree Fahrenheit, that's a Btu. Just think, a gallon of water is eight pounds! You take it from forty degrees up to eighty, and you've just stored three hundred twenty Btus! You know what this house's Q is?"

"What?"

"Three hundred twenty-five Btus!"

"Swell," she said. "How big a pool?"

"I'm thinking it should be about a couple of thousand gallons. Sixteen thousand pounds of water."

"How big is that?"

"As big," I answered boldly, "as the bottom half of a huge precast concrete septic tank."

This thought, this inspired conception, had the effect of propelling her to a state of complete alertness. "Hold on," she said. "Septic tank? Right in the middle of the house?"

"They cast these tanks in two pieces," I explained. "The top half has all the ports and baffles and clean-outs, but the bottom half is just a great big tub. A few tons of concrete, reinforced with

steel mesh — perfect! Perfect heat sink! First we pour the foundation, see. Then we have one of these giant crane trucks deliver the
tank bottom and set it down inside the cellar hole. Then we build
the house around it."

"I have heard of indoor pools," she told me, trying to be calm.
"But an indoor septic tank?"

"The genius of this," I said, "is it's just bound to be inexpensive. Because it doesn't have the word SOLAR stamped on it. Or SPA.
Or — just think, they make these things to bury in the ground!"

"I *am* thinking," she said. "I am thinking that a septic tank is
not my idea of a pool."

"Wait. Just wait and see," I promised.

In the morning, I phoned up the firm that has the concrete
concession in this broad valley. Almost without competition. They
are big on precast products: cellar stairs, cattle feed bunks, massive
horizontal silos. I said: "I am planning to build a new house on my
farm soon, and I need to know a little about precast septic tanks."

"How big a family?" asked the salesperson.

This struck me as an odd, almost an impertinent, question.
But I dutifully answered, two adults and two children.

"Two bathrooms? Laundry?"

"Wait a minute," I said.

"You on clay? Thousand-gallon tank should do it. One thousand gallons, that's our basic residential tank."

"Thanks," I said. "Except that isn't what I need to know."

"What else do you need to know?"

"What's the biggest size tank I could possibly get from you?"
"Huh?"

"Like, if I were a restaurant. Or a motel, say."

"Let me see here." The man paused to shuffle papers, dig out
spec sheets. "Twenty-five hundred gallons. We don't cast that
here, but we can get you one. But why?"

"Now, could I buy just the *bottom half* of that tank?"

"What is this, a joke?"

"I want to use it as a pool. Inside my house."

"You want the bottom half of a twenty-five-hundred-gallon
septic tank?"

"If you'll sell me that."

"Let me ask the boss," he said.

There was a substantial wait, while a conversation I can just imagine took place with the boss. Then the boss himself came on the phone. "I can do it," he said.

"What are the dimensions of that bottom half of the tank?"

"Says here, twelve feet long, eight feet wide, four feet deep."

I imagined such a pool of water sitting in my house, and liked it. "How much?"

"Six hundred ninety-three dollars, delivered."

Now that, I thought, sounds like a lot of money for half of a septic tank, but not much at all for an indoor pool and solar heat sink. "Sounds good to me," I said. "You suppose your crane truck can lower that tank into my cellar hole after the foundation's poured?"

"Should," he said. "When you going to pour?"

"A couple of weeks from now, depending on mud."

"Call back when you've got a foundation, and I'll send the crane truck out. Empty. Let the driver have a look-see. He should figure *some*thing out."

"Good," I said, and hung up the phone happily. Just a few days later, an old friend, who now builds classic New Jersey houses in New Jersey, dropped in for a visit while in Vermont for some end-of-season skiing. Eagerly I showed him the plans and models for my house, and told him about my septic tank/indoor pool.

"You can *do* that?" he demanded, incredulous.

"Of course, why not?"

"No *building code?*"

"In this little farming town," I told him with authentic pride, "if you own ten acres and you want to build a house, you have to do two things. You have to file a form that says how *big* it's going to be, and you have to pay five dollars."

My friend shook his head in disbelief. Then he started raising highly sensible objections. He calculated the weight of my pool, once filled, at twenty thousand pounds. Well over two hundred pounds per square foot of base. What kind of foundation would it take to support that load?

I walked him to the house site and showed him the smooth, hard, undulating ledge of the Champlain Valley running just a few feet underneath the topsoil. "I'll level that off with a yard or so of concrete, glue some Styrofoam onto it to create a thermal break, and have the tank set down right on top of it. Rock is rock, right?"

He nodded, with a trace of envy. "What about humidity?" he challenged.

"Humidity?" Now this was a new thought, and one that made me reminisce about growing up on the doorstep of the Pine Barrens. "Up here, our winters are mighty dry," I told him. "People boil water on their woodstoves all day long. And their furniture *still* cracks open at the joints."

"Maybe. Still, you put all that water inside your house — exposed — and you're apt to have moisture everywhere. On the windows, dripping . . . "

"Gee," I said. "A whole-house dehumidifier?"

"Try a half a dozen of them."

"Deck?" I brainstormed. "Pool cover?"

"Interfere with solar gain. And that's the whole point, right?"

"The point is building a little bit of Florida up here. Club Vermont."

"You might look into an air-to-air heat exchanger. Hot new item. Couple thousand bucks, though."

"What in hell's an air-to-air heat exchanger?"

"Like an open window — and a constant exhaust fan — but the heat in the air going out of the house is recovered and put into the air coming in. It's like an engineered system for infiltration. For modern, supertight houses."

"That sounds ridiculous," I said. "I can build this house as tight as I like, and then — if I need infiltration — all I have to do is hire one average carpenter to install one average window. Or — the hell, I bet this house is going to be so warm I'll keep a window cracked open. All winter long."

"If you can do that," he said, "you'll have humidity licked."

"And if I can't, if the whole indoor pool idea fails miserably, I will fill that septic tank with topsoil and grow banana trees. Or something. Point is, you only get one chance to set a chunk of mass like that inside your house. *Before* you start to build it."

And my friend agreed. "Thermal flywheel," he said. "It may not actively heat the house, but it would be damn hard for the house to ever get real cold."

He left the farm sharing a measure of my enthusiasm. But the man who went hog-wild for the idea was, of all people, the septic-tank delivery man who drove the concrete company's big crane truck. The day after my foundation was poured, he roared up the driveway and began crabbing around on the excavated dirt to find where he could set his stabilizer legs and maneuver the giant tank up over the side of the foundation wall and into the cellar hole. There were no logistical problems that he couldn't solve.

"Going to have that tank right in your house, huh?"

"As a *pool*."

"All the good tanks I have lowered in the ground," he said, with the remorse of a gravedigger. "And then watched a dozer bury them. This, I *like*."

"When can you bring out the tank?"

"It's fifty miles away," he said. "And my schedule's booked till Friday. But I . . ."

"*Friday?*" I had bought a pile of lumber, I had two skilled carpenters on deck to frame the house up with me, I had solved the last details and was itching to get building.

"Heck," the driver said. "You know, I'm just inclined to drop everything and get that tank for you. Job like this — and everybody's going to *see* that tank, right?"

"Built right into the floor," I assured him. "Come winter we'll go out and ski, then have a little swim . . ."

He picked up his radio and called in to the yard dispatcher. Some sort of emergency. He had to get the big tank right away. Simply couldn't wait. Then, with a wink and a grin, he crawled the crane truck off the soft ground at the building site and set off on his errand. Couple of hours later, he was back with the tank on board. With a maze of hydraulic arms and motorized cable winches, he set my indoor pool down on its marks in the cellar just as carefully as if it had been made of glass.

"Come on back and see it," I invited. "Once the house is built."

"You know, I think I might just do that."

Even my wife, who had had her doubts, admitted that the bottom half of a precast concrete septic tank can pass for a pool. It will pass a good deal better after I have had it tiled, and, sweat equity be damned, I will hire a mason to do that job. With mortar. It will need a pump and filter and other modern, sybaritic accessories; but as the house goes up all around it, Club Vermont looks better and better. Next winter, lounging at this spa while winter howls away outside, I imagine life won't seem so bad. I imagine I will think: in certain rare, inspired moments, one *can* make a silk purse out of a sow's ear.

CHAPTER FIVE

Adventures in Rural Living

*T*HE LAST THING I EXPECTED TO discover in rural living was a recurring sense of high adventure. I had expected to find peace and quiet. Stress-free living. Ample time for meditation. Yet, the way things turned out here, just going about the ordinary business of living often pumps me up with adrenaline. All about me lurk opportunities for heady risks. The unknown is my constant companion.

I strain now to recollect the things I used to find adventurous. Before moving to Vermont. One, I know, was driving a fast car at speeds somewhat faster than the speed limit. This is a young man's thrill, but what is apt to happen, really? Loss of license? Speeding ticket? The car that I used to drive was engineered for speeds considerably faster than those I ever pushed it to. It handled and steered and braked better at eighty miles per hour than my junker pickup ever did at forty. In fact, if a person in Vermont wants real driving excitement, he can purchase a car for less money than it takes to get a German sports car *tuned,* and careen all over our winding backroads at speeds that will never attract a policeman's notice. It will be every bit as thrilling as a flying Porsche. Slower, true; but who has anywhere to go?

I also used to find adventure by traveling to exotic places. Fact is, I still do; it's just my sense of the exotic that has mellowed with the passing years. I used to think that Greece was an exotic place; nowadays, Rutland will do nicely. It's not far away, but one doesn't go there at the drop of a hat. One plans ahead. One savors the experience. In Rutland, there's a shopping mall. They have a McDonald's and a Burger King and a Wendy's, too. They have buildings that are several stories high; why, some even have elevators. If one approaches Rutland from a properly rural — not to say barren — mindset, it can seem at least as exotic as Tahiti to a San Franciscan.

In my urban days, life used to afford continual adventure, as I risked victimization by criminal elements from which no one, in the modern city, can fully insulate himself. Car thieves, extortionists, muggers lurking in dark alleys — sharing an environment with such characters as these produced real fear, but it also managed to keep life exciting. In Vermont, a typical crime headline reads: TEENS BREAK INTO POOL, DOUSE CHAISE WITH BEER. The larger towns have actual cops, paid sleuths to investigate such heinous acts. Still, if that is your pool, and your chaise that reeks of stale brew, crime has scarred your life as surely as if you had been beaten in some subway station. It's just . . . well, much easier.

The last source of adventure I recall from my former life was the pursuit of trendiness, which is now called living in the fast lane. Going to the right places, wearing the right clothes, rubbing shoulders with famous or near-famous personages: that was exciting, but it was also an awful burden. Many play the game; few win. Most wind up staking a claim to being interesting people on the grounds that they have friends who are more interesting than themselves. This dubious form of adventure, at any rate, my wife and I kissed off completely when we settled in Vermont. Here there *is* no fast lane; most of our roads don't even give a person room to pass.

As compensation for the absence of trendiness — as though compensation were needed or desirable — the outstanding aspect of adventure in rural life is that a person, on his own chunk of real estate, can most often do whatever he damn well pleases. Vermonters believe in this state of affairs with a cross between religious fervor and gut instinct. Even when, in recent years, mandatory zoning of a modest sort has been imposed throughout the state, few citizens see any need for it to be imposed on *them*. Or their neighbors, either. If a person can't do as he pleases on his own land, then what is left of what this country used to stand for? Zoning is most often appreciated as a way of reining in the out-of-state development types.

On your property, if you think you'd like to raise a few thousand turkeys — why, just go ahead and do it. Nobody will try to stop you. Just *contemplating* such an enterprise is high adventure. If you want to build a pond, just hire in a bulldozer and figure out a way to pay for it. Trout? You can stock all the fish you want. You don't have to ask anyone — why *should* you need someone's permission?

This — after living in places where it took proof of residence to park one's car outside one's dwelling — this was adventurous stuff indeed.

And finally, there is the ultimate adventure of being on one's own. Yes, there are neighbors one can count on in time of need. Yes, there are minimal public services. But the sort of challenges posed by a blizzard — or a drought, or an inundation — are met initially by individuals working within the limits of their will and wits. Will the pipes freeze? Will the barn flood? Will the tractor start at twenty-four below? I know, I know — I lived for one year in Los Angeles, and adventure for me then meant merely *recognizing* Raquel Welch lunching at some posh hotel. No one could have told me then that adventure, *true* adventure, lay in trying to make a tractor start under the most adverse conditions. But I was wrong, then. And now I'm right — or so I like to think.

I know one thing: what you see depends on where you stand. From here, what I see is adventure beyond my wildest dreams.

• Sheep for Shore

Like many tracts of rural land, the Vermont acreage that my wife and I purchased was advertised as having a terrific pond site. Making such a claim costs a real-estate agent nothing, yet it can substantially enhance a property's description. Fishing, swimming, ice skating on my own country place — I could see myself adapting quickly to aquatic pleasures. A wiser person might have asked: What, exactly, *is* a pond site? But I refused to be so disingenuous, so mean-spirited a buyer.

What is a pond site? It turned out to be a place where one could, at phenomenal expense, engage a bulldozer to dig a hole.

Investigating pond construction — from the heady perspective of pond-site ownership — I discovered that there are three basic types of pond. The simplest, called a *dug-out*, is an utterly straightforward excavation to be filled in by runoff from the surrounding terrain. The second, somewhat trickier type of pond is called a *bypass:* one excavates near a stream or rivulet that can then be diverted to supply the pond once it is finished.

My site, however, cried out for the third and most sophisticated type of pond, the *embankment* variety. In it a stream is dammed directly. The way beavers do it. Any embankment pond is a ticklish proposition, fraught with hazards of design and construction. The site of an embankment pond is apt to be wet — where does a stream *go,* while one dams it off? — and wet clay can cause even heavy machinery to founder. Further complicating matters, my pond was to be a dramatic expansion of a stagnant muck-hole, where the stream that drains the farm meandered through a shallow meadow basin. Before digging anything, I had slippery mud to spare.

Even as a novice citizen-farmer, I knew that a person planning a pond ought to check in with the U.S. Soil Conservation Service. With good reason: in the good old days, this government agency liked to pick up the *tab* for farm ponds; and, even though that little bonanza has been zeroed out, the S.C.S. still gladly engineers such ponds for landowners. The government has noticed that dam failures cause profound soil conservation problems, so it wants to have folks build embankment ponds according to extremely conservative standards. This advice is free; following it can cost plenty. Still, I considered the engineering of my pond at taxpayers' expense to be a convincing bargain.

I first walked a Soil Conservation Service man around my pond site several years ago. He set up a transit level, then sent me scurrying up and down the muddy stream with a surveyor's rod while he noted elevations. "Heck of a site," he told me. "How much pond you want?"

I had an answer for him. I approach such projects with reasonably firm budgets. I had given this one careful thought. "Three thousand dollars," I told him expansively.

He laughed. "That should just about pay for the pipe."

"*What* pipe?"

He sketched for me, then, the government's approved embankment-pond design, which was predicated on a massive piece of plumbing. A vertical culvert, or standpipe, on the pond side of the dam would establish a maximum water level; any excess water would spill down into that standpipe and then be carried off through a horizontal culvert underneath the dam. The prescribed diameters of those heavy-gauge, galvanized-steel culverts were to be related to the maximum runoff that the government expected from my watershed once every one hundred years; in my case, after several sheets of complex calculations, thirty-six-inch culverts were found to be required. Ninety running feet of them. More steel than I might buy in a car or two.

"Gee," I said. "And how much for the bulldozing?"

"Rule of thumb, buck and a half per cubic yard of earth in the dam. I'd guess you're talking at least three thousand cubic yards, here. Plus any other shaping of the pond itself."

"Gee *whiz*." I was crestfallen.

"But it all depends. You get the right dozer in here, you hit the weather right, sometimes you can get a lot of dirt pushed in a few days. Then, on the other hand . . . well, I could tell you some pond-building horror stories. Make your hair stand on end. How deep is that little old muck-hole, there?"

"That?" I shrugged. "Couple of feet, I think. At most."

"Well, you'll have to drain that. First. I'd say put the dam right across where that muck is now. Give you pretty darn near an acre of pond. Ten or twelve feet deep — sounds pretty nice, huh?"

"Sounds like much more pond than I can possibly afford."

"That don't make no nevermind. We'll draw up these plans, and they'll keep fine until the year you're ready. Site like this, it doesn't make much sense to build some dinky puddle."

So I let his agency work up blueprints for a wondrous dam holding back a most substantial body of water. The embankment was to be well over two hundred feet long, and fully seventy feet wide at its base. The thousands of cubic yards of earth involved were to be scooped out of the bowl of the eventual pond, giving me considerable latitude in developing a pleasing shape. I chose a sort of huge teardrop. Then I was turned loose, with two nuggets of friendly advice, to find myself an excavator. Suggestion number one was: all things being equal, the bigger the bulldozer I could find the better off I'd likely be. Suggestion number two was: the more embankment ponds an operator had constructed, the less chance of trouble. Experience in such a tricky business counted for a lot.

Bulldozers in Vermont are generally in the hands of owner-operators who work for hourly fees that compare favorably to those charged by lawyers. Country lawyers, anyway. Almost all the fee, however, goes to make payments and repairs on the machines themselves, leaving operators with what amounts to a minimum wage. As a rule, the bigger dozers cost a good deal more to hire, but they have the lowest cost per cubic yard of earth moved. And the big machines have a valuable weight advantage: in building a dam, soil compaction is critical.

Training my sights, then, on the biggest machines, I made discreet inquiries for several years in hopes of finding a cash-desperate dozer jockey. Someone who would knock down his price considerably, or make an utterly unrealistic contract bid. No luck. Ponds, after all, are luxury items; those who want them built are expected to pay full fare.

Then, one rainy day in June a few years ago, a backhoe operator of considerable reputation knocked on my door. With his backhoe, I had heard it said, this man could all but change a baby's diapers. He was digging less and less with that machine, though, he told me. He had a new bulldozer. Bulldozers *create* things, he explained. They leave a landscape different. Backhoes mainly make a mess for bulldozers to shape up later.

I enjoyed this keen perspective, but it turned out he had not come to talk about machinery. He had come to talk sheep. He had a small flock, and he wanted to make it bigger. He wanted to know what animals I had for sale.

"Golly," I said. "How *big* a bulldozer?"

"Big. Second biggest dozer John Deere makes."

"How much are you digging for?"

"Fifty-five an hour. Plus the fuel."

"What a coincidence! I'm selling ewe lambs for fifty-five dollars, too. You . . . you ever built an embankment pond before?"

He shrugged. "Built quite a few manure lagoons."

Manure lagoons — for storing cow manure all year, in slurried form — are large, pondlike structures with embankment walls. But they do not usually have streams running through them at the time they're being built. Still, it sounded close enough for me. And too good to be true. We walked out to the barnyard, then we walked down to the pond site, and then we both went our separate ways to think. And I wound up swapping him some forty ewe lambs, the pick of that year's crop, for forty hours of pond construction with his dozer. Plus fuel. If the job ran any longer, I would settle up in cash; if shorter, he could settle up or I could take back lambs.

"That," I bragged to several friends, "is some kind of a deal."

"That," retorted one of them, "sounds like an unfair bidding practice. You're only considering excavators who want sheep."

"He's got the second biggest dozer made by . . . "

"You just better hope you don't get a manure lagoon!"

I confess I had a qualm or two along those lines, but swapping was the only way I could have seen the project through. And I sensed that all would turn out well on the bright Friday when he unloaded the massive dozer in my driveway, then trundled slowly across the meadow to my pond site. The ground beneath my feet shook — here was awesome power, here was strength enough to tame my little stream without scarcely breathing hard. If this was the operator's very first embankment pond, why, at least he was fired with enthusiasm at being about to join the ranks of serious shepherds. He would dig with inspiration. First, though, he needed fuel.

I had a fifty-gallon drum of diesel on my pickup truck — with a hand-cranked barrel pump — and with much effort I emptied it into his tank. Completely. There was lots of room left. "Say," I asked politely, "how much fuel does this dozer hold?"

"Seventy-five gallons."

"Wow! You must not have to fill it often."

"Once a day, generally. Pushing hard, she can drink at least eight gallons an hour."

I pondered these alarming facts as he channeled my stream away from the embankment site and then scalped the earth away from all around my little muck-hole. Child's play — at twelve bucks an hour in diesel fuel. Then the dozer waded right into that quiet, stagnant sink to shove it all downstream. Suddenly, ominously, the great machine paused. Then it settled gradually into saturated gumbo. The operator raised and dropped his heavy blade furiously; he gunned the engine and fought with the gearbox; and then he raised his hands toward heaven.

"Stuck!" he shouted to me over the motor's roar. He surely was — the glop was nearly up to his seat.

"What now?"

"Think you'd better try to get a backhoe in here. *Quick*, I think. Somebody to dig me out."

If getting a plumber in the city on a Sunday is difficult, try getting a backhoe in the country on short notice, late some Friday afternoon. I succeeded, though — it wasn't hard to make my voice sound frenzied on the telephone — and by sunset the dozer was back on firm ground. Saturday morning, *both* machines attacked the hole together: the hoe would fish out vile yuck by the bucketful, and the dozer would then run it across the landscape out of harm's way. That went on for many hours — and the backhoe jockey was not working for ewe lambs — till eventually the muckhole's depth exceeded the backhoe's seventeen-foot reach. No bottom in sight.

"Think this clay's been wet here for a good, long time," the dozer driver commented on his coffee break. Then — while I watched, aghast — he aimed the dozer down into the hole to shove glop toward the backhoe. Like heading for China. "No!" I yelled. "Don't do that!"

"Have to. This stuff's got to come out. We can't build a dam on stuff like this."

"But you'll just get stuck again."

He shrugged. He had been stuck before. When it came to getting stuck, he was cosmically stoic.

"What is the bulldozer worth?"

"Ninety-six thousand, new."

"And you — are you crazy? Taking it down there?"

"Got to. Backhoe can fish me out, most likely."

Half an hour later, my vaunted pond site was a moonscape with a huge dozer floundering around at the bottom of a crater, nearly out of sight. Crabbing over to fish out the bulldozer, the backhoe came frightfully close to falling in on top of it. I was sent to phone about trying to hustle in a *dragline*, if worst came to worst. A dragline is a tall crane, with cables that control a clamshell bucket — try getting hold of one of *those* on short notice, some Saturday afternoon. But then, miraculously, the bulldozer hit firm bottom. No more muck — just heavy, tractable, reasonably well-drained dirt.

I watched the big machine inch its way up from the grave. "That is going to make this pond some deep," I commented.

"No. We have to fill that in now. The embankment runs across that."

Fill it in he did, and then we laid the fancy culverts on firm soil of an appropriate type. And then, with the dirt going *his* way, as he put it, he spent several long days sculpting an embankment pond of remarkable beauty. Two million gallons, it can hold, and it took six months to fill. So what if my pond cost a little more green than I had figured on? It seemed worth it in the end. Everyone was mightily impressed with the result: friends, neighbors, Soil Conservation personnel, and even the dozer jockey, who came near to burying himself alive in it.

Then an older farmer up the road came down to see. Standing a good hundred yards from the standpipe that whisks away excess water, he asked: "Thirty-six-inch culvert?"

"Gee," I said. "You've got sharp eyes."

"You think that'll take the flow?"

"Think? I don't *have* to think. The *government* designed this pond. They sized that pipe for me. And anyway, this same stream flows beneath the town road through a thirty-six-inch culvert. And it's carrying more water when it gets there, right? And even in the worst spring runoff, we never see water standing up over the road, do we?"

The man listened patiently, then gave me a smile of amusement and of . . . well, of faint anticipation. He said: "Oh, I guess we did. In March of 1947."

Hundred-year flood? I hope it holds off for a few more years. I want to enjoy my pond before it's just a site again.

• Avian Angler

Not long after our pond was built, my wife and I attended the annual bash of some fellow sheep farmers who live several mountains away in Vermont's Northeast Kingdom. In the sticks, as it were. It was the sort of grab-bag party where a hundred social debts are repaid at a single stroke; accordingly, there were activities to suit all tastes. On the lawn were croquet, volleyball, and badminton. In the house, teenagers watched rock videos in the den, while dour, taciturn Vermonters watched blue movies in the basement. At one of three ponds (my friend *owns his own* bulldozer), there was swimming and snorkeling. And everywhere, of course, was beer.

But the most remarkable pleasure this event afforded — remarkable to me, at any rate — was that any guest could commandeer a fishing pole, carry it to the backyard *trout* pond, and haul up a few rainbows. Or a few *dozen* of them. Private pond. Stocked. No limit. Then one could slap one's fresh catch down on the barbecue and cook up a memorable delicacy on the spot.

This, I thought, is living.

When I got back home, I walked around my own pond and examined it critically. It looked just too new, too sterile and barren. The seed that I had broadcast to hold the banks against erosion had barely taken hold. And, because the pond required several months of rain to fill, every storm or passing shower churned up clay along the banks and turned the water chocolate brown.

"You going to swim in that mud?" visitors would ask me.

"After it settles out. It's bound to . . . sooner or later."

"Going to stock it?"

"Maybe. Maybe get some trout and put them in."

This comment invariably caused the listener to talk trout — to make some declaration or offer wise advice, the point of which was always that his trout knowledge exceeded mine. One would tell me: "Rainbow trout won't live in there. Too warm. Get yourself some brookies." Another would say: "Not enough oxygen in that pond for brookies." A third would warn: "Brown trout might do well there, but you wouldn't want them. Cannibals. And they're mighty hard to catch."

Soon I had a wealth of unsolicited information. Did I want my trout to spawn? Well then, I had better spread a load of gravel on the ice, come winter, and let it drop onto the pond floor come spring thaw. Did I expect fish to find a meal in a brand-new pond, at an infantile stage of ecological development? Sorry, I would have to buy Purina Trout Chow at the local feed store and toss some to the fish each day, till an authentic food chain could get established. Then there were the acid-rain zealots, who would shake their heads, Cassandra-like, and tell me to start liming the water after every rainfall. Otherwise, low pH would kill off everything in sight.

Overburdened with advice, I became discouraged about my pond's possibilities for aquaculture. Fishing might be great fun, but managing a finicky trout population sounded like something less than recreation. It sounded like an awful lot of work. And so I did not bestir myself to go acquire fish.

But it was astonishing how quickly natural forces began conspiring to colonize the pond — or to overrun it. Frogs and turtles and crayfish moved right in, including one monstrous snapping turtle that might, I imagined, gobble off a swimmer's toe without a second thought. And soon there was evidence of muskrats tunneling the banks. Weeds began to take root in the shallows, and to push their stems up well above the water's surface. Dragonflies and horseflies and mosquitoes found congenial digs. In short, the place was fast becoming wild.

This was what I had thought I wanted, but now it disturbed me somewhat. Unlike the trout pond at my fellow shepherd's farm, mine was not exactly in the backyard. It fact, it was a good quarter mile from my house — making it a pleasant destination for a daily stroll, but hardly close enough for humans to exert much supervision over what was going on there. And frankly, without denigrating Mother Nature, I was not pleased to see her latch onto this remote, attractive spot — a spot on which I'd lavished considerable time and money — as one more arena in which to try running amok.

So I set out to civilize the pond. I ordered fifty cubic yards of sand brought in — four groaning dump-truck loads — to create a beach. Furnished, naturally, with beach chairs. I built a marvelous hexagonal gazebo, replete with French doors and screens, so that cocktails or picnics could be enjoyed with minimal interference from bloodthirsty mosquitoes. I even bought a gas barbecue, so that lamb chops could be grilled down by the water on a warm summer's eve. Each of these improvements served to carve out a corner of the pond for the use of people, a safe place where wild creatures dare not tread.

Yes, it was the good life. Sunday mornings we could sunbathe — nude, if we liked — on the beach with the *New York Times*.

When pressures of rural life became intolerable, one could curl up with a good book down in the gazebo. Some nights we would float around the pond in giant inner tubes, just drifting aimlessly, clutching gin and tonics. But deep in my heart I knew that something was awry, amiss. This was not an ultimate sort of pond: it had no fish.

Then, one day, I received a letter from the government. A highly specialized branch of government, to be sure: the Otter Creek Natural Resources Conservation District, affiliated with the U.S. Soil Conservation Service. The gist of the letter was, did I want to buy some trout?

Now here, I thought, is government in action. At its very best. Jefferson would have approved: like the good king who worried whether his subjects were happy, here were public servants who wanted to rest assured that the pond-owning citizenry had adequate trout. A fish in every pan, right? For a mere forty dollars, I could buy one hundred rainbow fingerlings. Or brown trout, or brookies. Group order. Cheap. I could mix and match — or even order bass, if worst came to worst — and all I had to do was drive to Middlebury in a few weeks to pick up my purchase.

I called up an agent of the Soil Conservation Service, one who knew my pond quite well. He had helped design it. I asked, "You think trout would have a chance out here?"

"Never know until you try," he said. Wisely enough. And so I ordered three hundred fingerlings, half rainbow trout and half brookies.

Fund-raisers in these parts would probably pay dearly to obtain the mailing list of the Conservation District's pond stocking program. This is an upscale crowd. On a bright autumn day, I drove my junker pickup truck to town and stood in line with several dozen citizens, each of whom owned his own pond. Or several of them. Most also owned Saabs or Volvos or Mercedeses, the trunks of which were filled with cardboard packing boxes lined with newspapers or blankets. To transport their bagged trout in safety. They had purchased trout before; in fact, this was an annual outing. It was fish day.

I got in line and started talking trout with amiable strangers; as always, I gained new insights. How it takes a spring-fed pond to support brookies in the style to which they like to be accustomed. How rainbows will rise to take a fly when brown trout merely huddle on the bottom, wary. How, nevertheless, acid rain wipes out the rainbows first. Then I reached the head of the line, where two young men were scooping fish out of steel tanks and depositing them in large, clear plastic bags partially filled with water. One would grab the hose from an oxygen tank and pump the bag full; the other would deftly tie it off and, there, sir, are your trout.

I wound up with three bags — one hundred fingerlings in each — and arranged them on the truck seat next to me. They were guaranteed for just two hours, but I drove with patient care; one false move, and the truck's cab would have been a fishy mess. As it was, the trout splashed and darted about wildly in their plastic aquaria. Plainly, they were in a state of panic. What in their former lives could have prepared them for such a journey?

Arriving at the pond, I floated each bag in shallow water for fifteen minutes, till the temperature of the water in the bags matched that of the pond. Then, following directions, I sliced the bags open with a sharp knife and let the fish flow out into their new home. A very few trout took right off like bats out of hell; most dropped to the bottom like stones or lay on their sides looking shocked and bewildered. Then, at random intervals, each in turn would snap out of its trance and race off toward deep water. Soon the whole lot of them were engaged in frolicsome aerobic dancing all across the pond's surface, and I watched in sheer delight. Now I had a fishing hole.

Of course, I knew the trout would need a year to grow up to pan size. I was prepared to wait. I would get a casting rod, learn how to tie flies, and practice. Come next summer, I could count on many quiet hours of the sheerest relaxation.

A few weeks after my trout deal, however, my young son ran into the house and shouted that he had just seen a vulture at the pond. I doubted this. My son has an active imagination. Next morning, though, my wife reported nearly the same thing: she had seen a *heron* hanging out near the gazebo. Great. Blue. I took a walk and, sure enough, there was this absolute 747 of a bird cruising the pond. Magnificent. Wingspread just as broad as an eagle's.

My first response was one of immense pride — pride at having created a habitat worthy of this rare and magisterial bird's keen notice. I thought we should maybe call the Audubon Society. Host a little ornithological outing. Give the local birders something nice to check off on their Life Lists.

Before I could reach them, though, an angler friend dropped by to visit. Expert at fly-tying. Sort of guy who stops the car whenever there's a dead something-or-other at the roadside, to collect a bit of fur or feathers for some future fly. Sort of guy who wades into a stream, examines what insects are hatching on that given day, and sits down to tie something similar. I took this sportsman down to my pond to show him jumping trout, but they were not jumping. Not at all. Then he pointed to some tracks on the muddy bank.

"You've got a heron," he said.

"Great," I answered proudly. "Blue."

"Must be eating pretty well."

"Huh?"

"Herons are *fishing* birds, don't you know? Swallow trout whole. And fingerlings — they aren't smart enough to dive when a big bird hits the water."

"Gee," I said. "You think he might have eaten many?"

"You've got him on welfare," said the angler. "How many trout did you put in?"

"Three hundred."

"I give him six weeks to clean you out."

So I did not call the Audubon Society. I called the Soil Conservation Service, and demanded: "How do I prevent a great blue heron from filching all my trout?"

"Heron?" the government man repeated. "Trouble. Herons are protected. Migratory Bird Treaty. Course, if *I* had a heron feeding in my trout pond he wouldn't be protected very long. But according to the law, killing a heron is a federal offense. Can't you maybe chase it away?"

"This bird," I said, "is as big as my wife."

"Can't you scare it off?"

"It's more like the other way around."

"Well," he said, "then my advice is stock some bigger trout. Next year. Grown-up trout can usually dodge the birds."

"Thanks," I told him sadly.

The government gives, and the government takes away. I did not break a federal law; our heron dined with great distinction for about six weeks, then took off for parts unknown in a substantially fatter condition than when he arrived. I haven't seen a trout jump since, and have no present plans to restock the pond. But whenever I am challenged to do something kind or nice for our feathered friends — to build a winter feeder, say, or roll up little balls of suet — I plan to recall the gourmet spread I gave a heron, once. Hundred twenty dollars worth of mighty fancy bird feed.

• Crime in the Roads

A couple of years ago, I spent a few days in New York City: wide-eyed at urban wickedness, and with one hand firmly on my wallet. I avoided being victimized by criminal elements, but upon returning to Vermont I very nearly missed my driveway. It was late, and dark, but there was something wrong. Something missing. I blinked, and my large rural mailbox became conspicuous by its absence.

I thought: flee the simple life for one long weekend, and just look what happens.

Had it been in winter, I would merely have toted up another victim for the new wing plows that have made the town's snow removal trucks considerably more efficient. These hydraulic side-arms, operated by a crewman riding shotgun, have a way of uprooting even large posts effortlessly, and can sweep hapless mailboxes into snowbanks that are not apt to melt till spring. But this was October. There was no snow. Most probably, I figured, some speeding car had left the pavement and toppled my box into the roadside ditch. I made a mental note to go retrieve it first thing in the morning.

But when morning came, a thorough search turned up no mailbox. No *post*, either — and I had come to use a sturdy hemlock six-by-six to fend off reckless wing plows. All I could find, in fact, was the deep hole in the ground where my mailbox had stood.

"It's been ripped out," I told my wife.

"You mean ripped off?"

"That, too." But the expression grated on my lips; it recalled events — and a fearful attitude toward experience — that I had just about forgotten. Things are not often stolen in rural Vermont. Dimly I remembered sunstruck days in California, where my Porsche's Blaupunkt radio was ripped off three times in four months. Vaguely I could recollect a season spent in Boston — holed up on the back side of Beacon Hill — where several elaborate security locks were unable to foil petty thieves. I recalled, too, my little house near Philadelphia: how it had once been most professionally entered, loss of stereo resulting.

I had been ripped off before, in my nonrural past. I had had to look out for the things I owned and valued; I had organized my life to thwart those who were out to rob me. Lights went on and off by timers, locks were changed when keys were lost, but all of that was long ago. Ripped off in *Vermont?* Of my *mailbox?* It was nearly past comprehension.

Everyone has read that rural crime is on the increase. This is not surprising, since rural crimes are ridiculously easy to commit. Living in a place like this, the protective instinct for one's possessions quickly atrophies. Our society is small and ingrown; the anonymity that nurtures a criminal persona does not exist here. And our society is wonderfully coherent: the chances of anyone's starving or becoming rich are relatively slim. We lack a desperate element; we lack the greed and nihilism that inspire criminals elsewhere. All these traits make us sitting ducks for pros.

But pros are few and far between, and they don't steal mailboxes. As a crime victim, I thought that I should check in with the authorities somewhere; my town is far too small, however, to have a policeman. We have a hard enough time paying for a part-time town clerk.

"Why not call her?" my wife suggested.

So I did. I reported to the town clerk that my mailbox had been ripped off.

"So?" she asked.

"I just thought you'd know what I should do about it."

"Better call the post office," she suggested. "Right away."

That seemed like a good idea. I thanked her, hung up, and quickly reached the postmaster for the rural route I live on. "Someone got me good," I told him. "Took the box, the hemlock post, everything."

He was very sorry to hear it. "Federal offense," he muttered darkly. "Tampering with a mailbox. Was there any mail in it?"

"I don't know. There should have been. I've been away a few days."

"Mail theft's a federal offense, too."

This was reassuring — I could just see federal agents getting on the case. "What should I do next?" I asked him.

"Better get yourself a new mailbox, I reckon."

Somehow, I expected a little more of government. But I drove to town and shelled out $23.95 for a new rural box large enough to hold a good-size parcel or two. On the way, I reflected on our fragile and wide-open way of life here. On my farm are seven significant buildings, each of which must contain a few things of real value. Not only do we not lock doors, the doors don't even *have* locks; and it would be quite a little chore to retrofit all of them with the rudiments of security. The only keys I own are those I need to start my truck and tractor. The tractor key has never left the machine's ignition switch; and it takes an act of outright paranoia to pocket the truck key when I park in town. Why would someone steal my truck? It's *mine*, after all, and everybody knows it. Everyone knows everybody else's pickup truck; a successful thief would have to drive out of the county fast.

I drove home, past dozens of unprotected farms and houses. Somewhere in that placid, trusting landscape lurked a mailbox thief. A rotten apple. But the chances that I'd come across him seemed mighty slim. Maybe next year it would be china, not mailboxes. Maybe home furnishings, or heavy appliances. The average house around here could be ransacked in broad daylight; maybe the wanton theft of my mailbox marked the beginning of the end of something.

I was setting up the new mailbox when the postman arrived. "Something happen to your old one?" he asked.

"Stolen. Ripped off. Mail and all, as far as I can tell."

He rubbed his chin. "It was right here on Saturday."

"Even the *post* was swiped."

"Goddamn kids today, don't you know? Always out celebrating. Sounds just like some kids' idea of a prank."

"Prank! It's supposed to be a federal offense! And besides, I haven't ever been robbed in Vermont. Have you?"

"No. But Vermont is getting filled up quick with people from New Jersey."

That shut me up — *I* am from New Jersey, among other places. I painted my name on the shiny, new mailbox and eventually forgot all about the old one. Months went by. A year, even. And then one day, out of the blue, the state police called.

"You the Mitchell — Box 264 — that had his mailbox stolen?"

"Why, I — yes! Whoever told you?"

"No one told us. We turned up about a hundred mailboxes in an old hay barn, last week. Think we know the kids who stole them. Trying to reach all the owners. You want to come down here and identify your mailbox?"

"Sure — hey, that's fantastic! I'll get down there right away!"

In a garage behind the state police barracks, in Middlebury, I was shown a mind-boggling cache of stolen mailboxes. "Why?" I asked.

"Just kids, you know."

I had no trouble recognizing mine. I signed a couple of papers, then picked it up to put into my truck. "Not just yet," the officer told me. "We need to keep these boxes till the trial. As evidence."

"When's the trial?"

"Coming up. One of these months."

So I went home empty-handed, having helped the wheels of justice turn. Quite a while later, I received a call telling me to come pick up my mailbox. I sent my wife; the state had won its case, she reported to me. Malicious mischief, or something, against a pair of juveniles. One hundred nineteen mailboxes swiped. The kids were penitent, and had agreed to make apologies to each of their crime victims.

"I'll believe that when I see it," I commented.

"They're supposed to offer to make restitution, too."

But having my mailbox back seemed like restitution enough. I put it in a corner of my workshop, to hold wayward wrenches, and many more months passed. Then, one summer night, nearly two years from the date of the crime, we were entertaining on our deck when a pickup truck even worse-looking than my old junker pulled slowly up the driveway. Two distinctly rough-looking young men climbed out and shuffled toward our little party.

"Who are those guys?" someone whispered.

"Probably just looking for directions."

They did not ask directions, though. They halted just off the deck, and one of them asked ominously: "Mister Mitchell here?"

I gulped. The hell? — this was Saturday night. Who had come to break my thumbs? But there was no hiding. I nodded, slowly, and stood up.

"We need to talk to you," said one.

"*Alone*," said the other.

Shaking now, I let them walk me around the corner of my

house. We stood there for several awkward moments, sizing up each other. "This is real hard for us to do," said the one.

"It isn't easy," said the other.

"*What* is it you have to do? And . . . and why to *me?*"

"Well, we're the . . . we took your mailbox, a coupla years ago."

I let out an involuntary sigh of relief. "You did?"

"And we sure are sorry. It was really dumb to do. I just don't know why we did it."

"Why *did* you do it?"

"It seemed like a good idea at the time," said the other.

"At the time," said the one, "we were pretty drunked up."

"Can we do something for you now?" asked the other. "To pay you back?"

"Gee, I guess not," I said. "I just appreciate you fellows stopping by. I can see you're sorry. So, that's it?"

"That's it," they nodded, and they turned to head back to their truck. I took a deep breath, felt my heart pound, and then the wild rush of adrenaline hit me. Like after a near-collision.

When I climbed back on the deck, everyone was happily surprised to see me in one piece. "*Who* was *that?*" the guests demanded.

"Just the local mailbox thieves, come back to apologize."

"See?" said my wife. "I said they would, sooner or later." Then she had to fill them in on the entire story.

"That must be a hard thing to do," said the company when she had finished.

"Yes," I said. "It certainly was."

Well, that's the police blotter on my first decade in Vermont. Crime is on the increase, no doubt about it. Social disintegration looms on the horizon; anomie lurks just around the corner. But next time these chaotic forces interrupt *my* peaceful life, I'm ready. I have an old, spare mailbox all set to go.

• Dark Victory

Every solid citizen, I like to imagine, carries in his breast a secret memory or two of getting away with murderously antisocial behavior. It need not be mailbox theft; it need not even be illegal.

My personal favorite is the night I put the lights out, every last one of them, at the very height of our annual county fair. Seen in its proper context, giving full weight to the importance of such gatherings in the delicate fabric of rural life, dousing the lights was arguably a heinous act. Anarchists could do no better. Yet I got away scot-free.

Oh, sure, it was just an accident. I had gone to fetch a pail of water for my pen of prize-winning sheep, and in doing so I casually aimed a garden hose at what turned out to be the electric service entrance for the entire fairgrounds. Sparks flew momentarily, and then the fifty-acre tract was plunged into total darkness.

I *am* a solid citizen. I pay my property taxes on the first of each October; I vote in all elections, however inconsequential; I give a few bucks to the volunteer fire department every time the boys come around to hit me up. But did I stand there waiting to accept the blame for drenching a gray box full of circuit breakers? No, sir. I dropped my water pail, dropped the hose, and sloped off into the night. Feeling powerful and bad — feeling just like a felon — I stalked across the fairgrounds to appreciate what I had wrought.

Thirty thousand souls live in my county of Vermont, and, on Friday night of the Addison County Fair and Field Days, a solid majority of them are apt to be at the fairgrounds. Hundreds of our citizens, from youthful 4-Hers to octogenarians, would rate Field Days a bigger holiday than Christmas; many of those responsible for the fair have all but dedicated their lives to its management. And now I, in my modest way, had managed to affect every one of them. I had pulled off an eclipse, a blackout.

Watching a community's response to calamity is always an enlightening experience, permitting skilled observers to take the measure of entire societies. Our fair, unlike many others, is a self-conscious celebration of rural wholesomeness, of a pastoral ideal that depicts those who till the soil as morally superior to those who live in cities. Luckier, too. Consistent with this ethos, our fair affords no beer tents or girlie shows or auto demolition derbies. Public intoxication — of any kind — is not only prohibited but simply not seen. The spiderweb of culture is drawn fairly tight, as evidenced by three full pages of rules and regulations published in the fair's thick program book. Now, though — under cover of sudden and enveloping darkness — would a sinister, long repressed wickedness seize our spirits? Would we turn to rioting and looting, to licentiousness?

Down at the tractor-pulling pad, no one seemed intent on vacating the packed grandstand. Customized behemoths sat becalmed, with no way to see where they were going and no public-address system to call forth contestants and interpret their efforts to the horde of spectators. But tractor pulling is perhaps the slowest sport ever invented, and its devotees are not unaccustomed to sitting patiently through interminable delays of one sort or another: sweeping flecks of rubber from the concrete pad, making subtle weight adjustments from one wheel to another, maneuvering an extra thousand pounds of concrete onto the steel boat each tractor must attempt to drag. Far from undercutting the solemn drama of this sport, my turning out the lights had merely introduced a new, philosophical element. Darkness. *Zen* tractor pulling, see? No tractor. No weight.

Over in the vast show tent, the annual fiddling contest had been well underway when the lights went out. It was *still* in progress. Somebody had scrounged a pair of candles to set on the stage; but when a person has been fiddling for six or seven decades, as these contestants plainly had, light is not required to make music. The audience seemed not to mind, either. It was . . . well, romantic. I slipped out to continue my tour.

Besides celebrating classic rural Americana, our fair is an exposition of incredibly productive dairy cattle and frightfully expensive farm machinery. Some of the cows crank out one hundred pounds of milk per day — that is to say, about twelve gallons — but my mishap with the garden hose had shut down the state-of-the-art milking parlor where cows disgorge their udders twice a day in public. Since it is unwise to interrupt a cow's milk letdown, half a dozen blue-ribbon bovines were now being milked by hand for perhaps the first time in their lives. Just like on a dairy farm in the good old days.

"Think we ought to bring out the generator?" I overheard one herdsman ask another.

"Nah. I heard they'll have it fixed soon."

"What the hell happened?"

"Heard some jerk hosed down the circuit breakers."

I heard myself called something I cannot repeat. "We ought to make *him* milk these cows," the fellow added.

"Say nobody caught the jerk. Say he dropped the hose and ran."

I pressed on, a thin smile of villainy playing on my lips. I headed for the broad avenue where machinery — millions of dollars' worth of cold steel — is annually arrayed for the inspection of wary farmers. This is called *technology transfer*, nowadays, and it has been a fundamental justification for agricultural fairs for at least the past forty years. Farmers are too busy with their chores to get out and around much; and they have a prudential but somewhat inefficient habit of getting stuck in their ways. Of doing things the same way year after year. Farm economists and agricultural planners find this mighty disheartening, since they measure progress in increased productivity per farm worker. Fairs, though, introduce this army-in-coveralls to new machines — and whole new *systems* of machinery. If only a few each year sign up to become much poorer but considerably more efficient, then the nation's general economic welfare has been served.

But you can't sell farm equipment in the dark. I picked my way through $60,000 tractors, $80,000 combines, and $100,000 forage harvesters. I even climbed up to sit in the cab of this last; no salesman accosted me. Nice. Executive-type seat, stereo with fancy tape deck, air conditioning. A guy could impress his girl up here, some date-night. But I couldn't keep from thinking that this tool cost a good deal more than my entire farm, including house and barns, machinery, livestock — the works.

Leaning back, setting my tired feet up on the steering wheel, a light of blinding revelation clobbered me. Farmers, I saw plainly, were just drowning in technology. Farmers needed somebody like me to take them back to basics. Excess technology, like this amazing rig I sat in, was the very culprit responsible for farmers' embarrassing capacity for overproduction. That in turn was bound to keep farm prices depressed to break-even levels — forever and for always — dooming these yeomen to a life perpetually on the brink of insolvency.

So I climbed down from that evil office-on-wheels. I turned from temptation. What the farmers needed, I vowed to prove, was a return to the horse. To the days of pitcher pumps and kerosene lamps. What they needed, I realized without a trace of self-justification, was an end to rural electrification. Something much like what I had just happened to engineer. I might be a pariah in my neighbors' eyes, a miscreant, a . . . well, all right, a *jerk*. But I was a prophet, too. It is never easy to show the masses the True Way. I trudged onward, shouldering my vast responsibilities.

The fair patrons most disappointed by my power outage were those standing in long lines to get on rides at the bustling midway. Tilt-a-Whirl, Scrambler, Ferris wheel — all were shut down. Shills gave up enticing local he-men to games of chance, to throwing darts at balloons or swinging a maul to make a bell ring. As for the operators of this show — ardent adolescents with slick hair and dark muscle-shirts, spending their summer on the road going from fair to fair — they could not have been happier. Their real work, apparently, was to cut as wide a swath as possible through the flower of our county's womanhood; a reprieve from the drudgery of manning their stations meant prime time in which to pursue *amour.*

All too soon, the chief electrician had rewired the circuit-breaker box. The lights came on, barely fifteen minutes after I had doused them. Cheers rose from every quarter of the fairgrounds; tractors revved to life on the pulling pad, the Ferris wheel started turning, and once again it was Friday night at the county fair.

And I had to give my neighbors in this sprawling valley high marks for deportment in time of crisis. Things might not have fared so well in Essex, I reflected — at the Champlain Valley Fair — where crowds of rural folk seemingly stunted by inbreeding stagger from beer tents to shows pandering to man's baser instincts. And I shuddered to think what would happen if a blackout ever struck the Tunbridge World's Fair, an annual all-out bash of which the saying goes: "See it with a bottle of whiskey and someone else's wife." No, our sober community of doughty farmers had acquitted itself very well indeed.

I shuffled past the Field Days office, where the electrician and his helpers were stowing their tools. "We got to move that service entrance next year," he informed a groundskeeper. "That's just ridiculous, having it so near the hydrant."

"Been right there for years. Nobody ever sprayed the thing before."

"Seems like every year there's more damn fools around here. Had to happen, sooner or later."

Quietly, quietly, I left the open window of the office and went to retrieve my bucket. Right there by the hose. I filled it with water for my pen of prize-winning sheep, and let them slake their thirsts.

The very next year, I came across a new rule in the Field Days

Program Book. Rule Number 38: "Any additional wiring must be done by our Field Days Electrician and may involve additional expense."

Indeed it might, I thought — but for whom? Solid citizen that I am, there is nothing so exhilarating as a clean getaway.

• Certified Vermont Turkey

For several decades, Vermont's agricultural economy has been a compelling example of too many eggs in a single basket — the basket being, in this case, a whopping milk pail. Quite sensibly, a concerted effort is now underway to diversify our farm production into nondairy fields; this phenomenon has brought about a renaissance for all sorts of offbeat crops. Alfalfa sprouts, for instance. Dried herbs and spices. Guaranteed organic carrots, fruits and nuts and little berries — there is even ginseng under cultivation, I am told.

Behind each of the New Age agricultural enterprises, I am sure that brave and hardworking visionaries are struggling to make their receipts balance expenses. Such is farming. But there are a few hot tickets in the current sweepstakes to find viable alternatives to milking cows, and one of them — unlikely though it seems — is a feathered creature whose very name brings forth smirks and denigrating laughter in polite company. A large and somewhat awkward bird that gobbles and goes: "E-I-E-I-O!" all the day long. Yes, Vermont turkeys are poised to move into the fast lane of our diversified farm economy.

I first encountered Vermont turkeys three or four years ago, on a foray to acquire extra hay to feed my flock of sheep through the coming winter. Following directions given freely at the general store, I aimed my pickup down a long driveway toward a distant barn. On my right, a low chicken-wire fence enclosed what might have once been a pasture; now there was no shred of vegetation. What there was, was turkeys — several hundred of them, anyway, all milling about in the Indian summer sunshine like bathers at a crowded beach. Some were preening, picking feathers; others were engaged in the most abstruse philosophical debates; a few stood with their impressive tail feathers spread out wide in the basic Thanksgiving pose.

Suddenly, my old truck hit a bump in the driveway — I was rubbernecking, after all, not watching the road — and its tired shocks bounced the frame violently. Instantly, every "E-I-E-I-O!" was interrupted. Every bird stopped in mid-gobble, dropped whatever he or she was doing, and came to abrupt attention; one thousand beady little eyes were trained on me. Would they now stampede, I wondered? Would they hurl themselves into the fence in classic turkey style, pushing and crowding one another to the point of suffocation?

They did not. Within moments, a sort of groupthink informed them it was just a tired pickup truck lurching down the drive, and life returned to normal. I found the hay I wanted, found the farmer who had advertised it, and purchased a load.

"Make a dollar, raising turkeys?" I inquired cautiously.

"Awful lot of feed goes in 'em."

Now, I was not speaking to a New Age farmer. I was speaking to a Vermonter, and since he had not said no, I took his answer for a yes. So I asked him, "Hard to keep?"

"They can be."

"Do they really stampede, like people say?"

He smiled wanly. "Turkeys do everything people say. It's all true, whatever you've heard."

I suspected that there might be quite a few dollars raising turkeys, since my informant seemed determined to discourage interest. So I asked: "What sort of price do you need to make raising turkeys worth your while?"

"Dollar twenty-five a pound, dressed."

I whistled. At the time, plain old turkeys could be bought at the grocery store for sixty cents a pound, and Butterballs were barely bringing eighty cents. What gives? I wondered. "Do you *get* your price?" I asked him boldly.

"I expect I will," he said.

"How? Why?"

He laughed. "These are *Vermont* turkeys."

There are times in the history of American culture when rural life has been largely portrayed as *hokey*, as a landscape unappealing to sophisticated persons, inhabited by simple-minded bumpkins toiling their lives away at dull, wearisome chores. The present era, however, sees the pendulum swinging toward its opposite extreme: we live in a period when rural life is idealized, and nowhere more so than in New England. In times like these, the same bumpkins are transformed in the public imagination into heroic yeomen, keepers of the flame of our traditional values, a living repository of both common sense and profound wisdom. And, in times like these, the bumpkins know how to exploit their situation and make a buck.

Why should a turkey, by virtue of its having been raised in Vermont, command twice the price of someone else's birds? Because Vermont turkeys are scarce, of course — for the time being — and because there is no scarcity of people with more money than brains. The turkeys are shipped into the state, as eggs or day-old poults, from someplace else; the grain they are fed is shipped into the state from someplace else. Only incidentally — by the circumstance of their tenancy here — are they a Vermont product. And yet that is quite enough to turn the emperor's-new-clothes trick. In fact, it is *more* than enough: for many years, pork has been trucked into Vermont from the Corn Belt, smoked here with corn cobs, and sold at handsome prices as Vermont Smoked Hams. We smoke 'em right here, folks. Because the name *Vermont* can sell an awful lot of meat.

The turkeys, unlike the hams, are bona fide tenants here, for whatever that is worth; and tenancy requires a landlord. I expect that the typical Vermont turkey grower is unlike his out-of-state (and, most often, southern) counterpart. I have met a woman, for example, who numbers her turkeys in mere dozens and provides each morning some new divertissement to keep them interested in existence and spare them from the depressing social diseases that afflict bored birds all too easily: picking off each other's feathers, pulling feed out of each other's mouths, endless exercises in domination and submission. This concerned and conscientious grower will toss a beach ball into her birds' cage; next day, it will be a large mirror for them to preen in front of. Day after that, perhaps she will offer them an armful of wild ferns to investigate.

By Thanksgiving, these lucky turkeys can be touted as having had a variety of educational and sanity-nurturing experiences, despite having been reared in confinement. They will be sold as *Vermont* turkeys, at a dollar and sixty cents per pound, dressed. And who am I to say they won't taste different — more intelligent, say — than generic turkeys?

I asked this woman: "Is it true that turkeys try to lay their eggs while standing up? And thereby break them?"

She laughed. "I imagine every turkey story you have ever heard is true."

Another acquaintance just joined the turkey boom this past year, putting one hundred poults into an old shed no longer deemed structurally sound enough to store machinery. I watched him build a *round* pen; where there are corners, he explained to me, baby turkeys are apt to pile up and crush each other. I spent an hour watching him patiently teach each bird to eat and drink; otherwise, he explained to me, baby turkeys are apt to starve. Or dehydrate. These were not especially retarded birds, either. "Figure to make a killing on these?" I asked the fellow.

"Fresh Vermont turkeys always bring a nice, fat price, come Thanksgiving."

"Why?" I asked him pointedly. "Besides the fact that Vermont turkey growers are all slightly crazy, why should these birds . . . "

"It's the climate."

"The *climate!*" Now, this fellow had acquired his poults early in the month of May, when springtime is in high gear throughout most of the land. In Vermont, though, farmers are still waiting for the last frost. *Snow* can fly. There are no gaudy rhododendrons, no azaleas heralding warm weather — why, my friend had just installed a complicated and not inexpensive brooder to keep his birds from succumbing to pneumonia. I said, "If there is an ideal climate for growing turkeys, it must be far south of here!"

"Wrong," he said. "The cold makes them lay down subcutaneous fat. Which gives them flavor, see? It's like making a natural Butterball."

"What a line," I said.

"It's a *good* line. It may even be the truth."

I checked in with him some months later, smack in the dog days of August. It was not a time for laying down subcutaneous fat; but ninety-four of his birds had successfully learned to eat and drink and keep from getting smushed by their compatriots. One of them had learned to try to rape little girls, so my friend urged me to leave my daughter in the truck. His *own* daughter wouldn't go anywhere near the turkeys.

"E-I-E-I-O!" they gobbled at me, craning their pastel-colored necks in the air. Each sported a delicate, pink proboscis on its forehead and a flappy wattle at its throat. They were weird, all right — but they were graceful, too. And evidently they had been growing like weeds. My friend clapped his hands, and the birds — all but a few who were sleeping on their roosts — turned to give him their complete and undivided attention.

"This," I said, "could really stroke a megalomaniac."

"This," he said, "is wonderful."

"Is it true that turkeys . . ." I began.

"All true. All true. Whatever you've heard."

"How you going to sell these birds?"

"Just take out a small ad in the paper, come Thanksgiving. 'Fresh Vermont Turkeys, $1.75 per pound.'"

"Go on," I scoffed. "No one buys turkey at a price like that."

"You would be surprised. These are mighty well-fed birds. Mighty good eating."

"People like the taste of the name Vermont, I guess."

"Nothing wrong with that, is there?"

"Actually, no," I said. "By the way, where was it you said you bought these turkeys?" I confess: I had my mental calculator running. A dollar seventy-five is quite a price for dressed poultry at the farm gate. "I was just thinking, maybe sometime next year I might . . ."

His eyes crinkled with pleasure; he had made another convert to the growing ranks of turkeymen. But fate managed to interrupt my initiation. Somehow, one of the roosting birds fell off its roost. Like a child falling out of bed. Heat stroke? Overeating? It fell like a feathered stone — smack on its proboscis — and the impact sent the other ninety-three birds into a communal dither. Eventually they talked it out; the diving bird recovered its aplomb and went to eat some corn.

"That was lucky," said my friend. "Had one break its neck a few days ago, just that way."

"That *was* lucky," I said, offering silent thanks. "I was just starting to get interested. Now, though — don't get me wrong. The profit margin sounds fantastic. But I just don't think I want to worry about things like . . . like *that*."

My friend nodded, understanding. "Fine eating, come Thanksgiving. But Vermont turkeys . . . well, by any other name, I don't suppose they'd taste as sweet."

• A Christmas Carol

In the cities and suburbs where I grew up, the Christmas season started promptly on the day after Thanksgiving. Crèches were erected, doors sprouted wreaths and holly, Santa Claus arrived at the local shopping mall, and the air was filled with caroling and holiday greetings.

As a child, I did not complain. But when my personality began to assume something like adult proportions, I discovered that five straight weeks of joy-to-the-world was too much joy for me. I liked Christmas — I was not a Scrooge — but I would have liked it better if I could just be *surprised* by it. So I set out to de-emphasize the holiday season and to minimize its disruptive influence on my life.

Parenthood dashes many high ideals, though. As a parent, I have found my goal of a quickie Christmas is just incompatible with a crucial purpose of the holiday in our culture. Christmas is *about* anticipation, about teaching children how to master the intolerable wait for what has become an arbitrary date on the calendar of commerce. In thirty-seven days, we tell them, you're going to be very, very happy. Just try to stand it! The longer our society can manage to stretch out the buildup, the greater the lesson for our children in delayed gratification.

Still, I have had some success in minimizing the amount of merriment and goodwill that Christmas forces on my life. Living in a rural setting helps, as does living without television. Whole categories of holiday duty, such as sending out greeting cards or stringing colored lights to the pitched eaves of my house, I have managed to eliminate. After several years of getting no response, few friends persist in sending me *their* cards, either. This saves many a pang of embarrassment. But when the long Christmas season comes down to the wire — when there are, say, only two shopping days left, then I look up and drink in Christmas with a grateful heart. All the more grateful, too, knowing it will soon be done and past.

This is how I celebrate Christmas, nowadays: on December 23rd or so, I bestir myself and sally forth to purchase just a few essential presents. When these must be sent to their recipients, they will arrive weeks late; but it would pain me too much to shop any sooner, and, besides, in the sticks one can always blame the postal service for any delay.

On December 24th, as chilly dusk is settling in, my family bundles up and trudges through our snowy woodlot to find a young white pine tree, which I then chop down. We take turns dragging the thing home. Christmas Eve is spent lavishing many boxes full of gaudy decorations on it — in Christmas trees, I somehow feel, gaudier means better. When the tree is dripping with tinsel and colored balls, we set presents beneath it and put the kids to bed.

On December 25th, we carry on in pretty much the grand American manner, even postponing barn chores by a couple of hours. Then, amid new toys and dirty breakfast dishes, we commence preparing a Christmas dinner such as only a shepherd or a king can have: whole boneless leg of lamb, stuffed and baked inside a brioche pastry. Although a shepherd's family has to chew its way through several cull ewes and runty lambs in the course of a year, for this occasion we treat ourselves to meat so youthful, so tender and pink — so *prime* — that I doubt its quality could be obtained in a retail butcher market. Everybody helps prepare this *pièce de résistance:* my son mashes spices, my daughter kneads the pastry dough, I bone the leg with a razor-sharp knife. My wife directs and organizes all this activity, then pops the culinary feat into the hot oven. By the time family and friends arrive for Christmas dinner, the house smells like a five-star restaurant. *Gigot Farci En Croûte.*

We eat, and that is Christmas here: a feast. I like it very much. But just a year or so ago, a Dickensian Christmas ghost determined to smite me for my dedicated efforts to attenuate the holidays. Looking back, it looms in memory as *Le Noël Sans Gigot,* a non-Christmas from which I am only just recovering.

One pleasant aspect of spending Christmas in Vermont is that snow can usually be counted on — not the gray, wet, sticky stuff that falls on Northeastern cities, but the white powder of sleigh rides and sledding parties. In the year that I got mine, though, Christmas Eve brought in a howling blizzard. And on Christmas morning three *feet* of new snow blanketed everything in sight. Currier and Ives? Yes, but usually snow occurs at moderate temperatures: twenty-five to thirty-five degrees Fahrenheit. *This* Christmas morning started out at five below, and as the sun rose in the sky the temperature kept dropping.

We heat our house with wood, and I would not stint on

burning enough split oak and shagbark hickory to assure a toasty-warm living room on Christmas Day. The radio, however, carried urgent warnings from the power company that unusual demand caused by auxiliary heaters and Christmas tree lights was apt to result in brownouts, or worse. So, against my children's howls of protest, I unplugged the tree. Then I had to abdicate my ritual boning-of-leg-of-lamb act, in order to get the tractor started and clear the driveway. We were expecting several cars full of cele-brants, and they had to have more than a snowdrift to roll into when they reached our mailbox.

Real Vermonters, it is now well known, do not have long driveways. But I do, and the tractor I rely on to keep it clear was parked in a sheep barn toward the very end of it. Six hundred feet, say, from where the town road runs past my farm. Just walking to the barn took a considerable effort, and then I had to walk all the way back for a shovel to make it possible to open the barn door. Inside, I found soon enough, was an engine so tired and cold — so lacking in the Christmas spirit — that my usual cunning efforts to coax it to start were doomed to failure.

Intake manifold preheat: zilch.

Decompression knob: no discernible effect.

Glow-plug activation: nyet. And as I ran each of these cold-weather starting procedures, I could hear the battery mining its small quotient of sprightliness. On my last try, the starter went guuuh-guuuh-guuuuuuuh. And stopped.

A lesser — and more sensible — man might at this point have given up and shoveled out a portion of his driveway by hand, then enjoyed Christmas. But I saw the frozen tractor as a special chal-lenge, and in fact I was grateful to have the leisure time that a holiday affords in order to confront the problem. Why, that very morning my Christmas present had been a complete set of open-end wrenches. So I brought these to the barn and, at fifteen below, tore the battery out of my tractor.

"What's *that* thing here for?" my wife asked when I lugged the heavy battery home and set it on the kitchen counter.

"Needs a little charge. And it needs to be warmed up, too; cold engines need more juice to crank them over, but cold batteries have less to give. See?" I did not tell her that, for all practical purposes, the battery was drained of power. She, however, point-ed out the ice in four of the six cells when I unscrewed the caps.

"Take that dirty battery out of the kitchen, would you?" she suggested. "We're cooking here."

But I had a different plan; I set the oven thermostat to WARM and carefully placed the battery inside it. Then I went back to the barn to drain the oil from the tractor's crankcase.

"Now, just wait a minute!" she said when I returned with frostbitten cheeks and a large enameled vessel filled with oil so cold that it flowed like molasses. "You take that gunk out of here!"

"You can't expect an engine to start," I protested, "when the oil's thick as taffy."

"Honestly, take that . . ."

"I'm just going to warm it on the stove. Look, you're still boning. You're not cooking yet."

"I'm not going to *want* to cook. Can't you *smell* that?"

"Sorry," I said. "Company's coming soon. Got to clear the driveway."

I put my ski parka back on and went to drain the radiator of its antifreeze. When I carried *that* in — in the stainless steel pressure canner — my calm and patient wife lost her last vestige of equanimity. "These are not seasonings!" she hollered. "Battery acid, crankcase oil, and — now what's that stuff?"

"Ethylene glycol. Look, try to understand. I heat the coolant, pour it back, and then it heats the engine block. Cold engines are *hard* to start, but . . ."

Just then the power went off. As had been predicted. It is hard to get Christmas-spirited consumers to save electricity on their big holiday; pushed to its limit, something in the local grid had snapped. Outside the wind howled.

"You're not cooking anymore," my wife said. "Maybe I'm not, either. Meantime, though, get your tractor's innards out of this kitchen."

I could not but agree, and I noted that my wife had just one more compelling argument for changing over from electric cooking to a gas range. I hauled the battery out of the oven and carried it to the hearth near our woodstove; and I went back to lift the pan of crankcase oil off the burner. Which is when something terrible happened.

That pan of oil was hot — *hot*. I might have expected this, might have used thick potholders. But my hands were partly numb; by the time I realized that they were getting burned, they were *really* getting burned. "Christmas!" I yelled, or words to that effect, and then I . . .

Yes. I dropped the pot. *Gigot Farci En L'Huile Noir.* Which does not smell like a five-star restaurant. It smells like a . . . well, it smells like a service station.

Never even got the old tractor running, either. After squandering most of Christmas Day on the project, I gave up and shoveled out a few feet near the mailbox by hand. At twenty-four below. By that time, though, it felt positively pleasant to be out of the house.

The guests, when they arrived, were surprised to find spaghetti as the entrée of our Christmas feast.

So there *is* a Ghost of Christmas Past, and I watch my step whenever I am tempted to publicly minimize this important holiday. Even in Vermont, where folks like to imagine they are competent to make things work — to triumph over mechanical and climatic circumstances however difficult — even here, one begs for trouble by ignoring Christmas Day to try to start a dead machine. I have learned, when Christmas rolls around, to sing out "Joy to the World" just as loudly as the next fellow. I have learned to show respect.

CHAPTER SIX

The Perfection of Character

*I*TOOK MY FAMILY TO EASTERN Quebec a few summers ago, on a camping vacation. We entered the province well out on the Gaspé Peninsula, where the St. Lawrence River is too wide to see across. It was a Sunday afternoon, and we needed to purchase groceries for dinner before finding a campground.

In a little French-Canadian town, I parked the car and stepped out to accost a woman on the sidewalk with the sentence I had been composing, with utmost care, for the past thirty miles. "Pardon, madame," I began. "Est-ce qu'il y a une épicerie qui est ouvert sur le Dimanche?"

She stared at me. "Quoi?"

I swallowed hard and tried again — after all, I had studied French in school for many years. "Est-ce qu'il y a une épicerie . . ."

"Monsieur," she told me sharply. "Je ne parle pas anglais. Il faut que vous parlez français avec moi."

I climbed back in the car and drove off, badly shaken.

That is how it used to feel — almost every day, at first — when my wife and I came to settle in Vermont. Oh, the scenery was nice enough. The pace of life was great. The natives were not unfriendly. But it felt like no matter how I knocked myself out to speak a foreign language — a language of habits and concerns, as well as one of words — my efforts were deemed unintelligible.

Well, I *was* a queer bird. I remember a neighbor's kid helping me unpack some boxes — how he stared at the Compact Edition of the *Oxford English Dictionary* that I had purchased as a come-on offer from a book club. "Jeezum," he said, hefting it. "Weighs more than a bale of alfalfa hay." Then he saw the fine print, and the built-in magnifying glass, and he completely flipped. "You *read* this?" he demanded.

"With this dictionary," I explained to him affably, "a guy can *really* look up a word!" It was as though I was trying to say something like: "With this set of wrenches, you can really tune an engine!" I mean, I was trying to talk to him in a way I thought he'd understand. And I was trying to pass myself off as just an average guy, in spite of the fact that I possessed an O.E.D. These were serious mistakes, and they were symptomatic of a generalized need to apologize for my presence in this new community.

It took me some time to learn that apologies were not expected. No one is required to explain his presence in Vermont or to justify his likes and dislikes, whether they be dictionary or snowmobile. It took me even longer to learn that it was okay to be eccentric, or even irascible in a social situation. And that there was nothing wrong with running out of things to say; farmers who spend their lives conversing with machines and critters can get rusty at conversing with fellow human beings. That is called taciturnity by those who pride themselves on fluency, those whose conversations flow pleasantly along with a confident, internal logic. But over time, I learned that the taciturn are at least as likely to speak the truth as those whose conversations bubble abundantly.

The hardest thing to learn, because it required so much *un-*learning, was that a person's public self-presentation, in these parts, was not the only source or even the chief source of his feelings of self-worth. For people whose wellsprings of esteem and confidence are hard skills, practical abilities, and joy in work, those who focus their attention on a pleasing public image can seem rather shallow and inane. And when I realized that, I stopped trying so hard to pass. And gradually I became an individualistic cuss just like everybody else.

My French did not improve a whole lot during the Quebec vacation. But toward the end of the week I stood on a stone plaza overlooking Quebec City, and a pair of frumpy tourists from Texas came over to me. "Monsieur?" asked one.

"Oui."

"Is tha-at the Say-int Law-rence River over they-yer?"

"Yes," I said — in English, but it must have sounded like English as a second language.

"Thanks," they said. And as they left, one said to the other: "I'll bet that Frenchman would have said yes to *any*thing!"

Passing, in any foreign land or even in one's own, is an ultimate sort of thrill. In Vermont, it calls for the perfection of one's character rather than one's accent. Complicated business. But if one succeeds, he can take his place in a society of — what? Well, of perfect characters.

• Visual Acuity

I hadn't been long in Vermont before discovering that my neighbors saw things differently. I suggest no metaphor for difference of opinion; I mean that they literally saw things differently. And they saw things with a common sense that seemed at once deeply profound and utterly casual. I have, ever since, aspired to possess such visual acuity myself.

The first time I noticed this superior eyesight was on the day a neighbor watched me trundle manure uphill from my barn. In a wheelbarrow. "Up," he told me patiently, as though I were a moron, "is work."

Scales seemed to fall from my eyes, and I said: "I *see!*" But in fact I didn't see; I only understood a single, narrow application of the near-cosmic principle he had offered me. It was years before I could look out across a rural landscape and see endless crazy-quilts of *up* and *down*, see intricate patterns of potential work and potential loafing — or coasting, at any rate. Whether one is plowing fields, skidding logs, or baling hay, whether one is harvesting sap from a sugarbush or spreading lime or stretching fence, uphill is up. Is work. To appreciate this is to save many man-years of labor in the course of a rural life.

An interesting, advanced phenomenon related to *up* and

down is that these determine — absolutely — what path any drop of water will choose to take, rolling across one's farm in pursuit of bigger things: streams, rivers, mighty oceans. Of course, I knew before moving to Vermont that water runs downhill; but I could not read the dips and contours, the bluffs and gullies of a landscape as the history of water's incessant traffic. And I could not fathom how this history might shape the present. I could not see — as my neighbors could, by merely looking — what future aquatic calamities were inherent in any particular lay of the land.

When one sites a driveway, or a barn, or, God forbid, a house with no particular vision for what is apt to happen in event of too much water, one's myopia can imperil the most soundly built structure — or at least make life within it quite miserable for a time. Yet this business of the wise siting of farm buildings was, in my view, governed by radically different values. It was governed by a newcomer's respect for aesthetic principles, by a feeling for the essence of the rural picturesque. Would a building *look good* over there? was my sort of question. Would it afford its occupants attractive vistas? Even if the occupants were, say, sheep?

These were not the right questions. The right questions spring from a different sort of vision, one that can foresee how a hypothetical barn on a hypothetical site might behave under hurricane conditions, or come spring thaw, or in a good hard blow out of the northeast. Building with this sort of vision, a farmer not far from here sited his new house precisely in the lee of his broad dairy barn, notwithstanding that this placement blocked a hundred-mile view across Lake Champlain toward towering Adirondack peaks.

"Why?" I had to ask the man.

"Because it gets some windy on this rise," he answered.

"But that's a small price to pay. Think of the view you're missing!"

He said, "I have *seen* that view."

In fact he had — for thirty-seven years. Flatlanders dream of plopping down, drink in hand, to watch a mountain sunset through some broad expanse of Thermopane; those who live and work in this landscape every day, though, see things differently.

Seeing as they do, my neighbors were amused to watch me build a largish sheep barn on a site that, from their point of view, was headed for trouble. I nestled the structure smack against a steep hill, with underlying ledge erupting from the shallow soil here and there across the site. I *liked* the ledge; it obviated the arduous work of digging footings down beneath frost depth. But it also made a diversion ditch uphill from the barn impossible. I wished I had had such a ditch the very first time it rained; only with considerable effort did I manage to prevent the barn's inundation with each passing shower.

Then I found a worse problem; snow sliding off the building's vast, steel roof could, over a winter's time, create a massive dam along the downhill façade. Then, when spring thaw melted several acres of snow that lay *uphill* from the barn, its interior could become a lake of manure tea. I managed to build — I want to stress — a very lovely barn. While modern in design and in materials, it makes convincing reference to the fine tradition of owner-built Yankee agricultural structures. But its main floor would be more lovely, *far* more lovely, if it were not apt to be several inches underwater when my ewes are ready to start lambing.

"Look at that!" a neighbor of mine commented.

"What do I do now?"

"Raise the floor, I guess. Or go out and buy a pump. Water . . . you know, water always runs downhill."

"I see," I said. "I *see* that."

Eventually I hired a backhoe to solve these problems. Several hundred feet of trenches were dug, equipped with drainage lines and backfilled with crushed rock. Wherever depth-to-ledge permitted, the landscape around the barn was sculpted to divert stray water. Such site work is considerably easier and cheaper, though, when it is accomplished *before* one builds a structure. In fact, drying out my barn cost nearly as much as building it in the first place. It proved to be a powerful lesson in Vision.

Farmers have a legendary knack, too, for understanding weather; the ability of each of them to make sounder prognostications than, say, the National Weather Service is critical to their continuing solvency. I have noticed that my neighbors take a conservative approach to meteorological prediction. In the absence of any compelling new data, they presume the weather is less apt to change than it is to continue whatever pattern has been established. Even fickle weather can be perceived as such a pattern; the neat trick, though, is to guess when a given pattern is about to change. It doesn't happen often: entire seasons are customarily seen as wet or droughty, hot or cool, calm or breezy. The one thing a season can never be is "normal."

I had a different, more logical approach to weather when I moved upcountry. I possessed a meteorological chart based on thirty-two years of weather records at a station in this county; the chart set forth such interesting facts as that in June there are typically seven days with precipitation of 0.10 inch or more. (In June, too, the chances are pretty fair that precipitation will *not* take the form of snow.) Obviously, I thought, if it rained for five straight days in June, then the chances of rain falling on the sixth day would be considerably diminished. The Law of Averages, I thought, could wisely be applied to weather prediction by anyone who knew the odds.

I got my share of hay rained on by following this predictive strategy, but it was in a different context that I learned its fallacy. One summer, it *did* rain on five consecutive days in June. I was building a machinery shed, with a concrete floor, and I was pouring the slab in increments of two cubic yards per day — this was the limit of my strength, and of my little concrete mixer's. Each morning brought fine skies, and each afternoon brought a violent downpour just as I finished steel-trowelling the day's new concrete smooth. Driving rain can damage wet concrete considerably; my floor looked like it had a case of terminal acne.

On the sixth morning, the sixth *fine* morning, a neighbor came to visit. To examine my construction project. "Piece of work," he commented, examining my slab.

"I'll say! And the weather's been mighty uncooperative."

"Poor haying," he admitted.

"But I don't see any way that it could rain again today," I told him. "Just not possible."

"How's that?"

"Well, it's rained for five days in a row! It only rains hard for seven days in June, on average. There's a *Law* of Averages, you understand? Seven days in thirty; now, the chance of six in a row — see? Impossible."

He looked at the sky, a sky in which, I imagine, the first little clouds were forming. And he said: "Ayup. It sure rains easy, doesn't it?"

Sure enough, that afternoon brought a downpour. Right on schedule.

Little by little, I am learning to see the world through my neighbors' eyes. I am trying to adopt their specialized vision, since my own has gotten me into many kinds of trouble. Up is work, water runs downhill, rain falls easy when we're having a wet summer — these are early, simple lessons in visual acuity. By the time I'm ready for the big Eye Test in the sky, who can say how much more I will have learned to see?

• Government by Just Deserts

Government by town meeting is the quintessential Yankee political institution. In an age when Kafkaesque bureaucracies rule people's lives, one can't help getting misty-eyed at the thought of rural citizens dropping their work and trooping to their local town halls on the first Tuesday of each March to review, with a fine-tooth comb, the projects and budgets of their local government. Town Meeting Day, a statewide holiday in Vermont, is apt to fall precisely when a farmer should be tapping maples, getting set for sugar weather. Maybe there are fences to tighten, firewood to cut; everything stops, though, in order to perform what is touted as an exercise in grass-roots, no-nonsense democracy.

Transplanted to Vermont from points far south and west, I approached my first town meeting a decade ago with soaring expectations and a reverential spirit; what I witnessed, though, was an experience somewhat less than religious and bordering on the ignoble. Roughly two hundred grim, mean-spirited taxpayers crowded our modestly proportioned town hall, and quickly it became apparent that they had come to cut their tax bills.

Most of our town budget goes to pay for education, roughly divided between a union high school and our own elementary school. The latter institution of learning is called Beeman Academy. Most of the taxpayers in our town began their educational careers at Beeman, and a lot of them finished there, too. All those who manage to graduate belong, ipso facto, to the Beeman Academy Luminaries Society. The Luminaries hold an annual summer picnic. Beeman, an outsider surely might have thought, was dear to the town's heart; but the chairman of the three-member school board took the floor with evident fear and trembling. He unveiled a blackboard with a lot of numbers chalked on it — state aid, hot lunch, and so forth — but a hush fell across the room when he reached the bottom line.

"What it boils down to is this here — $122,000 from the taxpayers. Now, that's to run the whole school for next year. We think that's quite a bargain."

I thought it sounded like a bargain, too, especially since the town report in my hands indicated that Beeman had one hundred thirty pupils. Quick as you can say participatory democracy, though, a citizen in mud boots and parka was on his feet. The moderator recognized him. "Do you know," the man demanded, "how much that works out to cost per kid per year?"

"I think it's close to . . . well, is $900 close enough?"

"It is $938 per pupil. Now, do you know what they spend over in Otter Falls? Per pupil?"

"No, I don't. I guess you'd better go ahead and tell me."

"Only $850! And in Wrightsville it's only $835! And over in Monkburg . . . Monkburg gets the job done for only $790. Now, why are we spending $148 per pupil more?"

The citizen sat down to a smattering of applause. The school board chairman turned to his fellow board members to decide who would attempt a rebuttal. Leafing through the town report, I noted that these school board members each drew salaries of $150 per year. Something under three dollars a week — so why put up with this? They were, I had to suppose, dedicated Luminaries.

Now another school board member rose. "Beeman Academy is a considerably better school than what they have in Otter Falls or Wrightsville. Everybody knows that. On the standardized tests our kids always do better. When they go over to the union high school, Beeman kids are right on top. Beeman has a kindergarten, too, and that means we have an extra salary to pay. You won't find kindergartens in Otter Falls or Monkburg."

"Maybe we don't *need* a kindergarten," a citizen-farmer thundered. Then he looked up at the moderator to gain recognition. "Sure, a kindergarten may be nice to have, but times are hard. The cow is almost dry. Maybe we don't — here, just look at these here salaries in the town report. Thirty-four hundred dollars for a *music* teacher? Do we *need* a music teacher? Do we even *want* one? Kids sing well enough without one, don't they? Don't all these here frills like the music and the art — don't they get into the way of teaching just the basics? Don't we all want to get back to just plain old readin', 'ritin', and 'rithmetic?"

Now a citizen friendly to the school board's interests rose and took the floor. "Maybe it's true," he allowed, "that Monkburg runs their school for $790 per pupil. But did anybody here ever go on up to Monkburg? Ever *meet* those people? They come out of school and they can barely spell their names. Some might say they're very poorly educated. Some might even say they're dumb. Now, I don't think we want to make our town like Monkburg — do we?"

"Mr. Moderator!" An angry new voice was heard. "*I* come from Monkburg! Born and raised there. Went up through the schools. And I resent coming to town meeting to hear Monkburg folks called dumb! In Monkburg, we don't use grammar like 'these here salaries' and 'these here frills' — we use proper English!"

The moderator, a long-suffering man, intervened. "I'm going to have to ask you all to confine your remarks to the school budget and leave off debating the intelligence of people from various towns. Please. Now — yes?"

Another doughty farmer was recognized. "I see here on page 13 of the town report, it says we're going to raise the school principal's salary to $13,000. Now, how many of us in this room are making $13,000? Not very many, I'll bet you. *I'm* not making $13,000, that's for damn sure. Then you count up all the school vacations, and the snow days, the personal days, plus quitting work at three o'clock. Now, isn't $13,000 pretty darn extravagant?"

"Mr. Moderator? I move that we cut this school budget down to $800 per pupil, which works out to $104,000. Other towns can live with that, then so can we. Times are hard enough."

"Second that!"

The school board chairman stared up at the moderator, silently imploring him to exercise some parliamentary sleight-of-hand. He refused. He called the question. In an unmistakably clear voice vote, the townspeople chopped $18,000 from their school budget. In a rage, and out of order, the school board chairman rose and banged his fist on the little table. "Good for you!" he shouted to the citizens. "Congratulations! You've had your fun with the school budget now, and I hope you're just as tight-fisted when the selectmen ask you to buy a brand new dump truck! Good-bye!" He threw on his jacket and stormed out of the town hall.

There was a break, after the school budget debate, to let folks stretch and visit with each other and purchase coffee and doughnuts from some uniformed Boy Scouts in the back of the room. I *needed* some coffee — I found the angry tone and chintzy attitude of my fellow citizens to be simply shocking. In the line for coffee, though, a neighbor accosted me. "Well," he beamed, "how are you enjoying town meeting?"

I said, "Can we just *do* that? Cut the budget just like that?"

"Sure. But it won't do no harm."

"Cutting the budget by one-fifth won't harm the school?"

"Heck, no. They'll just call a special meeting in a couple of months, when the weather's warmed up so's people won't come. Then they'll have a reconsideration of what we just voted. They'll get all the Luminaries out to the special meeting, then they'll vote their money back."

"Then why," I couldn't help wondering aloud, "do we all come here and do this? If it's a charade . . . "

"Oh, we couldn't do without town meeting. Something to look forward to each winter, don't you know? Besides, if they're going to spend our tax money, we've got to let 'em know who's boss."

We? I thought. They? In my ideal of government by town meeting, such categories would have long since been obliterated. It would all be We The People. Our government. But the distinction between those who cough up tax money and those who spend it has proved extremely durable, whether government is by town meeting or by the fiat of some vast and impersonal bureaucracy of civil servants.

Sure enough, the meeting was called back to order to consider the selectmen's wish list for the year. They *did* want a dump truck — $28,000 worth of dump truck. And it turned out that farmers could well understand the pressing need for such an item. "Everybody knows," said one, "that when your machinery gets too old, all you have is trouble." The old truck had broken down three times that very winter, each time resulting in delayed snowplowing. Snowplowing can be mighty important to milk trucks and dairy farms. Besides, the new truck could be substantially purchased out of Federal Revenue Sharing funds, the governmental version of Santa Claus. The taxpayers voted to buy the town a new truck with scarcely a dissenting voice.

And then we got down to basics. Would we vote $300 to the town's Little League, for four dozen baseballs, forty-five caps, six athletic supporters, and a chest protector? Discussion of this weighty item took roughly as long as we had spent on the school budget. Were girls allowed to play in Little League? one equality-minded woman asked. Were we going to let the kids use the town hall bathrooms after baseball games? Would they trash the plumbing? Who would see to it that they didn't? If the Little League were truly nonsexist, if girls were allowed as equals, then should taxpayer money be spent on items like supporters? Important questions, questions that got right to the heart of local government. Finally, the town voted $300 for the Little League.

A dozen more requests for petty sums of cash were then deliberated, one by one. Would we give a hundred dollars to the Humane Society? How about fifty bucks to a local day-care center? Or $116.90 to the Otter Creek Natural Resources Council? On and on went the list of warrant items, an annual drama in which the townspeople could express their disdain for every sort of charity. The charities, for their part, seemed committed to devaluing the ideal of town-meeting government by making it into a fund-raising theater. Why? I asked a day-care representative of my acquaintance during the next coffee break.

"The money we pick up this way never comes to much," she admitted. "But we use it as evidence that all these various towns support us. Then we use *that* to go and get some real bucks. From the Feds or somebody. Get the picture?"

Yes. I did. The picture was that our charade was just part of a bigger one, involving government as it is practiced elsewhere.

Finally the selectmen got around to their budget, the one for keeping up the roads and running the town clerk's office and having use of a landfill — little stuff like that. Ninety-five thousand dollars. We voted them that not insubstantial sum with scarcely a murmur of discussion; and then, having discharged our civic duty for the year, we adjourned the meeting and drove home in our pickup trucks.

That was my first town meeting. A major disillusionment. In the many years since, there have been only minor deviations from the dominant themes I first heard on that frosty day. Sometimes we *do* pass the school budget as presented. Sometimes we make the selectmen give the volunteer fire department only two thousand dollars, rather than the three thousand they want. Every year we buy some big new machine: loader, grader, power shovel, backhoe, or the like. Every year we stiff the local charities and complain that education is no bargain. Every year we greet each other over tepid Boy Scout coffee, congratulating ourselves on our dedication to the tasks of citizenship.

Is it any better than government by bureaucrats? It is more accountable, for sure — but what tends to get unrelentingly accounted are the nickels and the dimes, the baseballs and the jockstraps, rather than the big-ticket items. It is not more *wise* than government by bureaucrats, in any case. Bureaucrats, God bless them, could scarcely do any worse.

But town meeting, I have come to feel, is a *fairer* form of government than its alternatives. Fairer, at least, for people like ourselves. Government by town meeting probably is not the best; but for we cussed, impossible Yankees, surely it is the government that we deserve.

• Leaf Consciousness

Twelve years ago, I spent a winter on a Greek isle, trying, I now suppose, to live the way I thought a young novelist ought to. The island in question was more than just another gorgeous, sun-struck Aegean jewel; it also was noted for the artistic flavor of its resident expatriate community. In many ways, my eventual escape to Vermont was a reaction to life in this art colony. Artists, I am sorry to report, are among the most difficult people on the face of the earth; a *community* of artists has not got much on a community of thieves and brigands.

And yet, I have noticed, Vermont and my Greek island share a most important feature: both attract seekers of idealized landscapes. This causes residents of both to flirt with the self-consciously picturesque, which can imperil beauty.

I remember one aging, dedicated painter who was a fixture on my Greek island's quay. He was not a great painter, nor one of particular reputation; but with quiet concentration he would attend his easel for several hours of each warm day, trying to render timeworn fishing boats — caïques — in a carefully subdued palette. He worked with a graceful, meditative discipline, and all he wanted while he painted was to be left undisturbed.

Every day at noon, though, a huge tour boat would steam into the port and disgorge a load of camera-clicking, free-spending vacationers — often, though not always, Americans. Sleepy merchants and taverna keepers would spring to life, throwing wide the shutters of the dozen bars and souvenir shops that lined the little harbor. Visiting these establishments would keep the eager tourists busy for a while; sooner or later, though, one of them would notice the old painter. Here was authentic local color. Here was something to be captured on film. Like as not, several tourists would sneak up on him at once, all bent on photographing Art In The Making.

"Say, are you a painter?" one would ask, startling him.

The old man would turn around slowly, deliberately. "What do you think?"

That would shut the visitors up, briefly. Not for long, though. "Oh, I get it!" someone else would crow. "You're trying to paint that boat over there, right?"

"You've got it," the painter would nod wearily.

"Think of that, a real painter! Do you ever sell them?"

"No."

"Then why . . . how . . ."

"I just do this," he would say with warmth and utter sarcasm, "to look quaint for folks like you."

I used to think this an uncharitable attitude — until, that is, I had relocated to Vermont and been through a few foliage seasons here. Vermont welcomes tourists on a nearly year-round basis, but most come here with straightforward demands that the state and her people can satisfy straightforwardly. Skiers want to ski; sportsmen want to land a few trout or maybe bag a deer; hikers come to trek the Long Trail or climb Camel's Hump. Visitors like these present no crisis of identity to the humble natives. The leaf-peeper, as we like to call our foliage viewers, is an altogether different species. Leaf-peepers come to find the pastoral, to wallow in a perceived essence of the rural picturesque. This can have significant psychic repercussions on those of us who live here.

True, we have developed a rough analog to souvenir shops and tavernas — predatory enterprises that snap to attention to welcome these visitors and help them make their wallets lighter; but there is something profoundly disorienting about having one's way of life deemed picturesque by a horde of vacationers from distant megalopoli. As if that were why we were *doing* it, after all.

As if the whole state were a sort of Sturbridge Village. I love the eye-assaulting foliage, our blazing maples just as much as anybody; but autumn has come to be a time when I find it hard to take my life and work and dreams at all seriously. Rather, I feel transformed into some minor detail of a Norman Rockwell painting. And I wonder: *Is* that why we do it? Merely to be picturesque?

I have clipped a snob ad from a snobbish magazine; the ad is on behalf of a "country cologne" called Devin. Here is an attractive couple — young, assured, on the make — dressed in expensive casual wear. They have parked their classic, foreign roadster by a white wooden fence on a winding country lane, and together they are trying to force a well-fed baby lamb to guzzle milk out of a bottle. The young man, smiling broadly, hugs the lamb tightly in his arms while his horsey girlfriend aims the bottle at its unrelentingly pursed lips. They are both very happy. "Everything you go to the country for," the copy reads.

That is how life seems, here, in the riotous height of autumn. *I* know what this handsome young man is going to find on his cardigan when he puts that poor lamb down. It isn't going to smell like "the country side of elegance," either. But the conceit that rural life is an endless tapestry of such resplendent moments — nourishing baby lambs, pressing apples into cider, splitting oak to stoke hot stoves on frosty October mornings — this is a powerful fiction, capable of disturbing even a seasoned Vermonter's dry-eyed perception of his daily life.

Not surprisingly, many chafe at being cast into the role of simple paisans in the Yankee hinterlands. Many bite the hands that feed them, one way or another. I know an old-timer who hangs a sign outside his house and tries to hawk his maple syrup crop at tourist prices. His sign announces:

GALLONS	$17.00
HALF-GALLONS	10.50
QUARTS	6.50
PINTS	3.95
HALF-PINTS	2.50

But those who pull into his driveway learn that he's all out of gallons. All out of half-gallons, too. And quarts. Still, some will assemble a gallon of syrup in pint and half-pint units, which, after all, come in attractive gift containers. Once the customer has handed over, let's say, thirty-eight dollars for a gallon of maple syrup, the sly farmer will look him in the eye and ask: "*Now* what do you think of us stupid Vermonters?"

Needless to say, this is not approved behavior. Citizens are coached by spokesmen for our tourist industry to be more warm, polite, and welcoming. Down-home radio announcers in sleepy towns read "foliage reports" on the air, right next to weather forecasts. "Maples nearing full peak on U.S. Route 4 between Killington and Woodstock," they will broadcast sonorously. One can almost hear an army of visitors dash to start their engines and go have a look. Feeding and accommodating this peripatetic swarm of humanity — in *any* style, let alone that to which they are accustomed — presents major logistical challenges to a state that boasts a mere half-million residents. It doesn't take many Scenicruiser busloads to overwhelm a little burg blessed with a few too many breathtaking sugar maples.

Chambers of commerce sometimes try to stem this tide by finding rooms for roomless leaf-peepers in the homes of proud Vermonters looking for a few spare bucks. This gives rise to real feats of hands-across-the-seamanship, as visitors and visitees strive to understand each other. A commercial beef producer that I am acquainted with took on some foliage viewers last year, and all went well until one of the tourists asked if he could go out to the barn with him. To maybe break some hay bales open, maybe help him out a bit with his evening chores.

"What do you do for a living?" asked my friend.

"Why, I'm an attorney."

"Well, how would you like it if I dropped by your office and tried to help *you* out with chores? Maybe write a few letters to some of your clients, or . . . "

"Oh, my work is far too . . . too *specialized* for that."

"So is mine!" the farmer burst out angrily. "Don't you see that? So is mine!"

I doubt that they closed the chasm these remarks opened up, but I also doubt that my friend put his finger on exactly what was bothering him. The truth is, our working lives here *are* picturesque, far more so than life in any law office. One cannot blame visitors for admiring and wanting to participate in what they regard as lovely; the upsetting thing is that through habit, through familiarity we have ceased to notice so much of the beauty that attracts outsiders. They look at a barn and see a harmony of man and nature, while the farmer sees hungry animals — again — and peeling paint. And the farmer cannot help but envy the visitors their fresh eyes, even while expressing annoyance that they cannot understand the complex human efforts that sustain such a landscape.

And the truth is worse than that. In order to recapture their appreciation of Vermont — in order to see for themselves what the tourists see — Vermonters are all too apt to build and landscape in styles that exaggerate our austere traditions. One can see this in both new and reconstructed buildings; one sees it most egregiously in a host of restaurants and motor inns and Olde General Stores that drip with fabricated versions of rusticity. Supposedly — but mistakenly — these excesses are thought to have appeal to outsiders. The truth is that the spectacle of Vermonters aping what is emblematic of Vermont cannot be very attractive to our thoughtful autumn visitors. A healthy society should not have to work so hard at self-presentation, should not try so hard to get its details right that it winds up overstating them.

The truth is what the old painter on the quay in Greece knew: when we are conscious of being watched, when we are perceived as quaint, the beauty and the art in our way of life is in grave danger.

Leaves drop, eventually; and a season without color clears Vermont of tourists until snow whitens the hills and valleys. Those who live in idealized, attractive landscapes need these barren seasons desperately — need to have times in each year when nobody is watching — to preserve a fragile cultural sanity, to recover a threatened self-confidence or nonchalance. Without these, even the leaf-peepers might stop coming; our autumnal pyrotechnics would not seem so splendid if Vermonters were to lose their collective soul. And ad writers would then have to find new images in order to sell cologne. So I'm thankful for Novembers — and Septembers, too. Without either one, Vermont would soon lose everything that folks go to the country for.

• Enforcer

One snowy winter morning I trekked to my barnyard and found a pair of dogs busily feasting on my sheep. On three of them, actually. The other ninety-seven stood huddling by the barnyard fence in the abstracted state that profound terror can somehow induce. It was as though they were wishing themselves nonexistent. Or at least invisible.

Every shepherd understands that, sooner or later, he will find himself in the middle of such a scene of carnage. Sheep are, after all, defenseless; and many breeds of canine have profoundly predatory and carnivorous instincts. But for eight years I had been spared even a single dog incident — I credited electric fences, and the virile presence of my own dog Breeze, who had come with the farm — and for those eight years I simply did not know how I would respond to seeing my sheep flayed alive.

Now I knew: I was at once livid and cunning. In accordance with my legal rights and some deep, unconscious impulse, I vowed I would kill those dogs.

The dogs, who bore a striking resemblance to wolves, looked up from their ambitious breakfast. They were wary of me, even though I acted as if nothing were amiss. I could not figure out how they had gained access to the barnyard, which is quite substantially fenced; for their part, they seemed unable to figure out how to escape. A nice situation. I ran the shocked survivors of that ambush into the barn, and closed the door behind them. And then I went to fetch a gun.

The gun, a basic, undistinguished rifle, had arrived on the farm several years after we did; it was in storage for my Texas brother-in-law. Pacifists by inclination and by temperament, my wife and I had hung the thing high up on a wall, and had not touched it since. Not only had I never aimed the weapon or fired it; it had no ammunition. But now, leaving the dogs to clean up their meal, I hauled the rifle down and threw it in my pickup truck and roared off to the nearest store that advertised "reloading tools."

If ever someone looked self-conscious carrying a gun, it was me walking into that sporting goods establishment. But I laid it on the counter, made believe I was John Wayne, and said boldly: "I need some ammo for this."

"Twenty-two?" the clerk asked.

Trouble was, I didn't really know. And when I said, "I think so," it changed the whole tenor of our little conversation.

I handed him the rifle. "Twenty-two," he nodded. "Do you . . . you know how to shoot this thing?"

"Actually, no," I said.

"Then what the hell you doing with it?"

"There's some dogs been bothering my sheep. I thought I'd show them something."

"Show them something! What you want's a shotgun, then. Buckshot. Give 'em lead."

"I haven't got a shotgun. I've got this."

"What are these, wild dogs?"

"They sure do *look* wild. Look like wolves. No tags or collars."

"Possible," he said. "Most likely someone owns them, though. People oughtn't let their dogs run, but plenty do. Anyway," he said, setting a box of bullets on the counter, "this ought to cure them of it. If you get your shot." Then, at considerable cost to the cowboy persona I was trying to affect, he showed me how to load and aim and fire a .22 rifle.

Back at the farm, I walked to the barnyard gate and shot both dogs dead. It didn't happen in a couple of shots — or in a couple of minutes — but after a few wild misses my Boy Scout Merit Badge training came back to me, and I buried years of nonviolence to canines with a pair of accurate, well-placed rounds. Then I went into the house to phone a town selectman, because by a nineteenth-century law Vermonters whose sheep are killed by dogs can proceed against their town for damages.

"Sure these aren't wild dogs?" asked the selectman. "Sure they aren't coyotes?"

"I have no idea what they are — or were," I said. "No tags. No collars. Look like wolves, sort of."

"Towns don't have to pay for the work of wild predators. Just domestic dogs."

"Well, come have a look," I said. "They're lying right here in my barnyard, next to three dead sheep."

The selectman arrived within ten minutes, and he was, in a way, impressed with my marksmanship. "They look domestic to me," he nodded. "Maybe crossed to something wild. But I'll bet somebody owned them. Anyway, I don't suppose they'll bother you again."

"The town will pay for my dead sheep?"

"I suppose we'll have to."

I didn't advertise the fact that I had killed two dogs, but word traveled fast. By nightfall, the owner of the dogs had called me. He was sorry; actually, we both were. The dogs *had* been one-quarter wolf. They weren't yet fully grown. He had planned to train them to go hunting with him, someday, but they broke their chains and ran off and began behaving just like wolves. It was the first time they had gotten loose from his place. As for my shooting them, he said he would have done the same himself under the circumstances. No one in this landscape filled with valuable grazing livestock will defend a feral canine.

But the real upshot of that harrowing day was that I had to admit my old dog Breeze was no longer an effective deterrent to unwanted guests. I had, over several years, watched his sense of territory shrink from one hundred acres down to a mere backyard; but the kicker was, he had cowered in the machinery shed throughout this entire dog attack and shown no interest whatsoever in taking on the intruders. This simply could never have happened in the years when he was in his prime. How much simpler, I thought, for dogs to fend each other off than for people to have to shoot them.

So when I received the town's compensation for my sheep, I went out shopping for a new guard dog. Very quickly I was steered toward a breed called Great Pyrenees, a French dog used for many centuries to guard sheep flocks. Pyrenees grow big — one hundred thirty pounds would set no record — and after attaching themselves to a farm and flock, they will defend them fearlessly against anything from traveling salesmen to grizzly bears. Pyrenees are all-white and long-haired; from a distance one might almost pass for a sheep. But their almond eyes are rimmed in deepest black, and lips and nose are also jet black. Reared up, tail flying, standing its ground and barking away in *basso profundo*, a Pyrenees dog creates a presence of incontrovertible authority.

Purebred Pyrenees dogs, though, are not cheap. Three to four hundred dollars is the going price — for a *pup*, which may or may not turn out successfully as a working guard dog. Pyrenees are scarce, too: a reputable breeder is apt to place a customer on a long waiting list pending some distant whelping.

"How can we afford a four-hundred-dollar dog?" my wife asked — except she wasn't asking. "And just think what it's going to eat! You don't grow one hundred thirty pounds of dog on table scraps."

She was right. I had a plan, however. I said: "Look, we'll buy a *female* Pyrenees and breed her in a year or two. Then we'll be right out there selling four-hundred-dollar puppies ourselves."

"Dog breeding isn't all that easy," she remarked. "And neither is raising pups. And as for selling them for four hundred dollars — people who can pull that off must live, eat, and breathe dogs."

But I had made my mind up; when I thought of my lost ewes, it seemed I could not afford *not* to have such an enforcer. Not long after, I journeyed several hundred miles to a kennel with some fancy pups for sale. Champion bloodlines. Five-generation pedigree. Show dog quality, but out of working parents. When I drove home, I had the puppy of my dreams curled up next to me.

The old enforcer, Breeze, had a canine version of a nervous breakdown. Not that he attacked the pup; but he began sneaking off, up and down the road, entering neighbors' houses to trash their wastebaskets and scare their kids. This was mighty dangerous, since I had made it known that I was prepared to live by the sword where other people's dogs were concerned. There were complaints. Finally, one single weekend, we heard from the town clerk, the Humane Society, and the Vermont State Police that old Breeze was a public nuisance. With a dog fourteen years of age, our options were limited, and after a few days' soul-searching we took him to be put to sleep.

The Pyrenees pup, however, had a solid year of growing up to do before she would acquire the relaxed temperament and maturity of judgment required for long days of roaming the pastures. In fact, for a long time she could not be trusted off a chain, and, when excited, she could break even a strong chain with alarming ease. In the house, it was worse: she grew big enough to eat off the *top* of the refrigerator. Nothing was safe. With a quick wag of her tail she could clear a couple of plates from the dining room table. Expressing affection for my three-year-old daughter, she would deck her and leave her bawling on the floor, half-trampled.

"That's a lot of dog," my neighbor commented the day she pulled over the plows I had attached her chain to. "You might get a harness for her. See if she'll do tillage work."

"She's *supposed* to calm down," I said. "She's *supposed* to guard the sheep."

"You get her to stay put in a pasture," he predicted, "and you won't see any other dogs around."

And the man was right, with one exception. Fully grown, my

Pyrenees mellowed out beautifully and began exhibiting classic guard-dog behavior, which is to say she affects a benign indifference toward the sheep themselves but walks my fences several times a day, barking her head off, leaving her scent behind, and generally declaring herself the local bouncer. Having walked her beat, she finds a shady spot to take a nap. She naps a lot: immense dogs like Pyrenees have an unfavorable ratio of body volume to surface, and this, plus her thick coat, make her uncomfortably hot much of the time. Uncomfortably hot, she finds a shady place and goes to sleep. But when a hundred-thirty-pound dog is napping in your pasture, the sheep who graze there have a potent insurance policy.

With, ahem, one exception. The morning came when I trekked to the barnyard and found dogs hanging about everywhere. Big dogs, small dogs, purebreds, mongrels; inside the fence stood my Pyrenees, torn between her instinct to guard the flock and some new, profounder instinct. She had come in heat — in fact, before this pack of suitors, she was transformed into a sort of canine Marilyn Monroe. A big blonde. Way off in the distance, I could see more pilgrims making their way toward my farm. True, they all had One Thing on their minds; but I had to fear that some disappointed lover might act out his amorous frustration on a sheep or lamb. Generally speaking, wandering dogs and sheep don't mix.

When is a guard dog not a guard dog? When it is Valentine's Day — when she is a female called to perform higher duties. I ran the sheep into the barn, ran the Pyrenees down Lover's Lane into the house, and spent the next few days chasing stray dogs off the premises. Meanwhile, I tracked down a couple of owners of stud dogs of breeding and distinction; even over the telephone, I received quite an education. Had my bitch been *shown?* Had she had her *hips* X-rayed? Would I like to sign a five-page contract covering a host of contingencies pursuant to getting done for my dog what any stray mooning in the backyard would have gladly done? And the cost — the cost of a service, with no guarantees expressed or implied — was four hundred dollars.

"What did I tell you?" asked my wife. "Don't mess with purebred dog people. They will beat you every time."

But I had a willing damsel who had excellent sheep-guarding qualities, so I pressed on and turned up a male who had been sold without the full nine yards of pedigree. Yes, he was a purebred dog; all he lacked were a few pieces of paper. For the promise of a pup, I arranged to borrow him for a long weekend, during which he and my dog wore each other out. Some months later, several fluffy, hamsterlike creatures hit the sunroom floor.

In my limited experience, but against received wisdom, the breeding and whelping of large canine breeds is no big deal. Certainly not compared to a frantic lambing season. But as for selling four-hundred-dollar pups, my wife had been completely right. Unless one's life is manifestly wrapped up in dog breeding, customers just laugh at you. I managed to clear some fifty bucks per puppy over costs — and the costs were quite considerable — which meant that, with eight pups, my guard dog actually recouped her purchase price for me. So I could tell my wife to stop complaining about my dog. But as for getting rich, it was not in the cards. Still, a dollar is a dollar.

I let my farm's enforcer hang out in the house for two straight months, savoring maternal pleasures; this was a mighty long time to let down my guard. But then, once the pups were weaned and disappearing one by one, Mom expressed profound resentment at being returned to her street cop beat. She wanted a house to live in. She wanted to be barefoot and pregnant. Following a flock of sheep around a sprawling pasture was no longer my dog's idea of a good time. In fact, she would leap my most respectable electric fence to leave the pasture and go out looking to meet some men.

"Awfully sorry about this," I said lamely to a neighbor several miles up the road, retrieving my dog after one of her unscheduled cruises.

"That's some big dog. You should keep her home."

"God knows I agree. Lately, though, she just won't stay."

"She had puppies?"

"Once."

"You ought to spay her. That'll slow her down."

Spay her? The thought had not occurred to me; I saw the dog as breeding stock. But when I investigated this piece of advice, I was surprised to learn that breeding a guard-dog bitch can ruin her completely for enforcement purposes. So I had a choice to make: did I want to hustle meager sums of money selling pups without being a dog fanatic, or did I want to provide protection for my sheep?

I called my veterinarian and arranged to have it taken out.

Getting along with canines is a source of tremendous satisfaction to countless human beings, but I am not particularly proud of my success at it. Like the young fellow at the sporting goods store told me: you can cure a stray dog of his feral instincts with a well-placed bullet. And if you would prefer to have your guard dog guard your sheep, you can cure romantic instincts with a couple of deft incisions. Really, though, is this fair? Is this the nature of our age-old compact with this attractive species? Sometimes I am shocked — shocked! — to think what tactics are employed to get along with man's best friend.

• Body Heat

Asserting my right to defend my sheep from feral dogs was a giant step in having my bid to pass as a Vermonter taken seriously — by me as much as anybody else. In other ways, though, I am afraid I've failed completely. Perfect characters are permitted to have perfect flaws; certain kinds of flaws, though, are hard to overlook. Certain kinds of flaws betray an utterly non-native core. In my case, an enduring failure of character surrounds the fact that I get cold.

Of all the odd arenas in which people stake out claims to being existential heroes — showing off wounds and incision scars, touting feats of long-distance driving or jogging, braggadocio concerning how much liquor one can drink — I imagine none is so universally popular as the mere survival of winter, or wintry weather. And this is a marvelously relative game, so much so that it can even be played in Florida after a night of frost. But in a place like Vermont, where winters last half the year and sorely test the human spirit, each person's ability to grapple with the chilly beast becomes a fundamental wellspring of self-respect.

Or lack of it. I thought that, in moving to Vermont and struggling through its heavy-duty winters, surely my claim to climatic heroism would be made secure; but I was mistaken. The pettiness and backbiting inherent in this business compelled Vermonters living north *and* south of the Champlain Valley to point out — correctly — that I live in the most temperate part of the state. Low in elevation and relatively flat, the extremes of cold in my corner of Vermont are moderated by proximity to a substantial body of water. When some acquaintance drops in from the Northeast Kingdom — or from Brattleboro, even — on a frigid January day, when outside it is a mere five degrees above, they are apt to cite their fortitude for living in a harsher climate. In fact, they are generally apt to carry on as if my farm were located somewhere near Cuernavaca.

That is not the way I see it. I abhor cold, and — besides having designed and built a marvelously warm, tight house — I have conceptualized a number of sensible inventions to counteract cold's worst effects. Why, for example, could not typewriter keyboards be equipped with heating elements and tiny fans to blow warm air up onto a typist's fingers? I would call *that* user-friendly. One can sit at the keyboard in a winter coat and hat — I used to do it all the time, in the old barn-house — but the fingers of a typist still stand naked to the office air. TypoHeat, my simple answer, will correct this problem as soon as venture capital is forthcoming.

And then there are winter days — even in the new house, sometimes — that are so bitter cold one wants to give up and crawl back into bed by ten A.M. Why, in all these centuries of northern culture, has nobody invented a simple device to turn the pages of a book propped up in one's lap, without having to withdraw one's hands from beneath the covers? This strikes me as a serious omission, one that I am working on.

My problem, of course, is a sedentary winter life. Sitting at a desk just does not work up the sweat that milking cows does, or felling trees, or driving a big truck on narrow, slippery roads. I have a twenty-minute barn chore each winter morning — feeding and watering my flock — and it takes me twenty minutes every evening, too, to haul in the next day's firewood from the outside pile; but apart from those brief forays into the bitter cold, I prefer experiencing winter from the *inside*, thank you. Long-time acquaintances from points south of Trenton may mistake me for a sort of champion at winter, but no one around here is fooled.

The bizarre thing about those whose work requires them to brave our winters out-of-doors is that they appear to have a pecking order based on how inadequately they can clothe themselves without ill effects. I first encountered this phenomenon early in my tenure here, when my pickup lost its fan belt on a snowy mountain road. Stopping at the nearest general store/

garage/liquor/gun establishment, I huddled by a coal stove as a mechanic clad in coveralls made the repair — outdoors. Then, as I was settling with him, in walked a pair of rugged men in *T-shirts.* One had the *sleeves* ripped off. True, they had merely walked from their car into the store to stock up on beer or ammunition or something; but I don't go *anywhere* so thinly clad in January.

"Jeezum," said one of them. "It's starting to turn cold out there."

"Think it's just a tad above zero," the mechanic told them.

"Nothing like last winter, though."

"Nope. I won't forget that one."

What had they had to do the year before, I wondered, shivering. Maybe wear shirts with sleeves?

Just a few weeks after this, a neighbor invited me to accompany him on his brand new snowmobile. My first ride, and last. Since the day was sunny and not bitterly cold, and since my chauffeur was only wearing a light jacket, I did not bundle up excessively for this adventure. But the wind-chill created by roaring across a frozen landscape at speeds that would get one arrested on the highway is nothing to be trifled with. After ten minutes I was hollering for mercy.

"What, you cold?"

"I'm getting frostbit. Numb."

"Me, I don't *get* cold," he assured me. As if I had some strange disease. "Feel my hand . . . go on, just feel it."

I took off my down-filled mittens to feel his hand, which was bare. His fingers were as warm as if we'd spent the last ten minutes rocking by the fire. And he wore no hat, though I was wearing a stocking cap and had pulled the hood up on my parka, too. "How?" I asked, amazed.

"Circulation's good, I guess. Always been this way. Hell, nothing's worse than being cold. So I . . . I just don't."

"I *do,*" I said.

But I never did toughen; on the other hand, my wife did. Never any fan of clothing, she did have to bolster her wardrobe of summery cotton dresses with wool skirts and sweaters — even stockings — when we first arrived here. But she quickly shed them, and by our second winter she was padding around our not-overly-heated house in flimsy embroidered blouses and thin chemises. And bare feet. This can really emasculate a man who needs a thermal T-shirt, turtleneck, and two sweaters to keep his chest from shivering.

She understood immediately, too, about the real Vermonters' gift for warmth. She said: "It's like *tumo*."

"*Tumo?*"

"In Tibetan Buddhism. *Tumo* is internal heat."

My wife had been dabbling for years with yoga exercises — standing on her head for a while each morning, and like that — and though I had tolerated this amusement I never dreamed it might have any practical application. Now, though, she produced for me a volume entitled *Magic and Mystery in Tibet*, written in the 1920s by a French anthropologist named Alexandra David-Neel. She flipped through it to a chapter called Psychic Sports, and had me read "The Art of Warming Oneself without Fire up in the Snows." This is certainly as worthy of study in Tibet as in rural New England. And the message, stripped of its religious wrappings, was very much the same as my snowmobiling neighbor told me: if a person vows to not feel cold, it can be avoided.

Tibetan Buddhists — and David-Neel became one, eventually — place themselves under the teaching of a master in order to learn *tumo*. Advanced breath control is an important qualification, as well as perfect mental concentration so that one can enter deep states of trance; my neighbors, it must be admitted, lack these credentials. But neither do they participate in the startling competitions that David-Neel writes about, in which graduate students of *tumo* spend a night squatting naked by a frozen lake or river. Handlers or referees chop a hole in the ice and dip Tibetan T-shirts into the water, which the spiritual athletes then wear till they have generated sufficient heat to dry them. Then they are dipped in again.

The winner of the contest is the one who dries the most T-shirts by morning, up to forty of them. But anyone who dries three T-shirts passes the exam and is thenceforth called a *respa*. *Respas* are a snap to spot, because they wear but a single cotton garment in all seasons and at any altitude, which is to say they dress just like my wife.

"This is just fantastic," I told my wife, handing the book back. "This is how you do it?"

"No. But it shows that keeping warm can be mind over matter. That's what these Vermonters do, I'll bet you."

"Well, I'm ready to sign up."

"For *tumo?*"

"I don't mean the frozen lake bit. I'd just like to be able to sit in my office on a cold day without a jacket on. And without my fingers freezing."

"Then you don't want *tumo* — there's some mighty fine print attached."

"Oh?"

She thumbed her well-worn volume, and read: "Once initiated, one must renounce all fur or woolen clothing and never approach the fire to warm oneself."

"Never? Never ever?"

She nodded.

"Well, I'd like to sign up for whatever class the neighbors took, then."

"They didn't take a class. They were just born here."

"And you? How do *you* do it?"

"Just warm-blooded, I suppose. And you're not. Face it. Find some other way to be a hero."

Warm blood may be a dominant trait; both of our children seem to have it. Then again, they both were *born* here. Maybe that's the answer. And, though growing up so far off the beaten track imposes certain cultural privations on a child, I was astonished recently to learn that my son's third-grade class was going to spend a morning with the Dalai Lama. Honestly, the spiritual leader of Tibet was visiting these parts, and he wanted to meet children.

"Ask him how he keeps warm," I advised my son. "Without fire. Up in the snows."

"Why should I ask that?"

"Because you'll maybe learn a thing or two."

Not surprisingly, the Dalai Lama showed up in a thin cotton garment to meet the Vermont children; my son wore a T-shirt with a couple of holes in it and one sleeve coming off. Everyone sat outdoors in the late autumn sunshine, eating apples and swapping stories, and I realized the great man had little to teach the kids about internal heat. Some are called to defy winter by the frozen lake, others to do so on the snowmobile or by feats of improper dress. And then there are some of us — neither from Tibet nor Vermont — who must huddle and shiver and stoke the stove. And pray for spring.